THE FOOD PROCESSOR COOKBOOK

THE FOOD PROCESSOR COOKBOOK

by Dorothy D. Sims,
director of the Culinary Arts Cooking School

New York • London • Tokyo

International Standard Book Number: 0-8256-3142-4
Library of Congress Catalog Card Number: 78-66437

Printed in the United States of America.

In Great Britain: Book Sales Ltd., 78 Newman Street, London W1.

In Canada: Gage Trade Publishing, P.O. Box 5000, 164 Commander Blvd.,
          Agincourt, Ontario M1S 3C7.

In Japan: Music Sales Corporation, 4-26-22 Jingumae, Shibuya-ku,
          Tokyo 150.

Book design by Geralyne Lewandowski
Cover photograph by Herbert Wise

Contents

The Food Processor Guide

The FOOD PROCESSOR is an assistant in the kitchen and not a gadget if used properly.

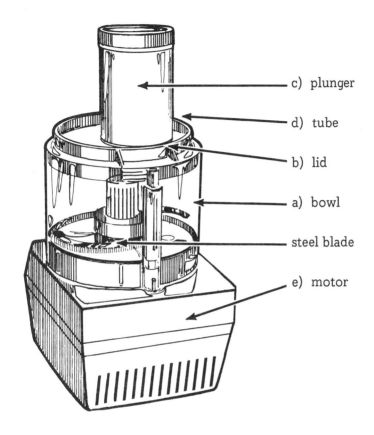

c) plunger

d) tube

b) lid

a) bowl

steel blade

e) motor

Keep the machine on the counter. The processor bowl is much easier and faster to clean than a cutting board.

The (a) bowl and (b) lid are made of Lexan and are dishwasher proof. The (c) plunger is made of hollow plastic and should not go into the dishwasher because it will warp and not fit into the (d) tube.

The spring is activated by the lid, which puts pressure on the white dot to start the motor. You never touch electrical wiring, so you do not have to be concerned if the processor bowl is damp—you will not hurt the machine or give yourself a tingle.

The motor (e) is permanently sealed and does not require maintenance. If the machine should require servicing, contact the manufacturer and provide the serial number, which is located under the base of the machine.

When working in the kitchen one always has moisture on the fingers. Instead of holding onto the disk and wiggling it into place, give it a little whirl and it will drop into place. This avoids slipping that might give you a nick here and there. Treat the disks and blade with respect—like any other sharp instrument.

To avoid nicks and cuts on the fingers, wash the blades with a bristle brush, then let them air dry in the blade holder or caddy.

Number One Safety Precaution: Always wait until the blades or disks have stopped revolving before removing the lid.

Remove the bowl from the machine before removing the blade. It will not cause any damage to your machine, and will save you one cleanup step.

Keep the motor on when working with large quantities of liquid to avoid leakage. When pouring liquids from the bowl, hold the blade in place with the spatula.

To avoid liquid running over the sides of the bowl or onto the shaft, keep the motor running until all the liquid is mixed. Turn off the motor and immediately remove the bowl from the machine. This will form a temporary seal.

Train your eyes. Viewing, not timing, will make the difference in the finished product.

Try working with the machine turned away from you. The leverage and visibility are substantially increased. When the machine is facing you, you have to look around the tube. When it is facing away from you, there is 90% visibility.

The on/off method produces an even texture, because it allows the food to drop down around the blades when the motor is turned off. You can process new particles of food continuously.

This machine is excellent for using up leftovers and making baby food.

When shopping, keep in mind the size of the processor tube. This can help eliminate a lot of waste. Draw the outline of the plunger on your grocery list and measure items while shopping until you are familiar with your machine.

The bowl has a 4-cup capacity. It can accommodate any recipe that calls for up to 3 cups of flour.

The tube holds 1 cup when filled.

When converting your own recipes for the machine, if leavening power is needed, add a pinch more baking powder or soda. If egg whites are the leavening agent, add an extra egg white. The machine works so fast it breaks down the leavening action.

Steel Blade

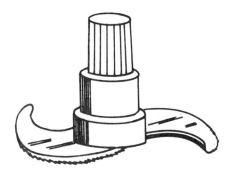

The STEEL BLADE is used when force is needed, for chopping, beating, and whipping, and for grating such items as Parmesan cheese.

TO CHOP ICE: Insert the blade and 1 or 2 cups of ice cubes. Use the on/off method. After a couple of spins of the blade, check that the blade is still in position. At times a cube will slide under the blade and lift it up. If this has happened, just wiggle the blade back down. Continue to chop the ice to the desired consistency. The ice can be used for caviar, mousse or shrimp cocktail base. It is also good for shaved ice, frozen drinks and Italian ices.

TO CHOP MEAT: Insert the blade and use the on/off method until the desired consistency is reached. Raw beef needs to be cut into small cubes before it goes into the processor. Cooked meats can remain in larger pieces. Remember the less you handle the meat, the more tender it will be.

TO BEAT EGG WHITES: Wash and dry the bowl and blade before using. Add a pinch of salt to the whites and beat. They will be transparent at first, then they will turn white and climb up the wall of the bowl. They then will start rolling like snow caps. Remove the blade, turn the bowl upside down and lo and behold—perfect egg whites. A maximum of 9 whites can be done at a time.

TO WHIP CREAM: Beat until the cream is the consistency of sour cream. Add the sugar and flavorings through the tube while the motor is running. When a rim forms around the bowl, the cream is ready to serve. Do not overbeat or you will have flavored butter. This butter cannot be served with bread, but it can be used in recipes when butter, sugar and the flavorings are called for, or it can be used for glazing sweet rolls and cakes. A nice thing about whipping cream with the machine is that all the spots are on the lid and not all over you.

FOR BUTTER: Beat the heavy cream until you hear or see the liquid. This is buttermilk separating from the butter. If salted butter is desired, add salt at this time and give the blade another turn or two. This does not hurt the buttermilk. If you want to make garlic or herb butter, remove the buttermilk first and add the flavoring.

If you have a recipe that calls for ½ cup cream, throw the remainder into the processor bowl and make butter. If you can't use the butter immediately, freeze it.

TO CHOP ONIONS: Use a fast on/off technique and the onions will chop, not liquify. Cut the onions in half before putting them in the processor bowl. Onions are easier to peel if cut in half first.

PARSLEY AND OTHER HERBS: Use the on/off method and chop. You can use the stems as well as the leaves because the machine chops them up equally well, providing more nutrition. Wring the herbs dry in cheesecloth or a linen towel. This will not damage the herbs, and they are now ready for the freezer or refrigerator. If you need more liquid to make green sauce or mayonnaise, a tablespoon of water can be added.

TO MAKE PEANUT BUTTER (or any nut butter): Use the on/off method to chop the nuts. Cover the blade with about 1 cup of nuts (more can be used if desired). If you want chunky nut butter, reserve some of the chopped nuts and add them after the butter has been made. Let the machine run, and a ball of paste will form. Remove it at this point if making almond paste or a filling for a layer cake. Let the machine run and it will go into the "peanut butter spin." The longer it runs, the oilier and smoother the butter becomes. When it reaches the desired stage, add the reserved nuts for chunky nut butter. The machine sends off puffs of smoke while processing nut butters, but do not be alarmed—this is caused by the friction of the nuts, not the machine overheating.

BROWN SUGAR: It sometimes gets hard sitting on the shelf. Do not despair! Throw it into the processor bowl and process until it is light and fluffy again.

EXTRA-FINE SUGAR: Granulated sugar will do the trick after a few turns of the steel blade. Process longer and it will produce powdered sugar. This should not be confused with confectioners' sugar, which contains 3% cornstarch.

BREAD CRUMBS: Save pieces of Italian, French or other hard breads. Use the steel blade and start with the on/off method a couple of times, then let it whirl. Four slices of bread yield 1 cup of crumbs.

Plastic Blade

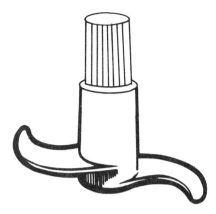

The PLASTIC BLADE is used for mixing and blending mayonnaise, hollandaise, and dips.

Because it does not change the texture of food, the plastic blade can be used to prepare chicken and tuna salads. It is also good for making bread crumbs from fresh, soft bread and for making cracker crumbs.

Shredding Disk

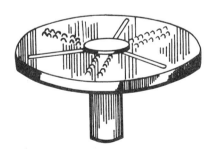

The SHREDDING DISK juliennes and shreds food that is fed through the tube horizontally; it grates food fed in vertically. To sliver almonds, lay them flat horizontally.

Slicing Disk

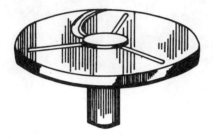

The SLICING DISK slices and juliennes.

When using celery or carrots for decorative purposes, cut pieces to the same length and pack the tube tightly to prevent tipping, which makes side slices.

The pressure used on the plunger determines the thickness of the slices. Heavy pressure gives thick slices; less pressure produces thinner slices. The food is sliced so fast all the goodness and liquid is maintained in the finished product.

CABBAGE: Slice with medium pressure for slaw.

TOMATOES: Cut in half and use heavy pressure.

ONIONS: Use small yellow or pearl onions and place them in the tube, stem end down, to make perfect little rings. Use heavy pressure.

MUSHROOMS: Use heavy pressure or they will crumble.

LETTUCE: To shred, use heavy pressure.

To make matchstick potatoes or to julienne celery root, use two steps. 1) Feed the tube vertically and slice, using heavy pressure. 2) Remove and stack the slices together. Then feed the tube horizontally and slice again, using heavy pressure.

Also use the slicing disk when making carrot, celery or any dip sticks by feeding the tube horizontally.

Optional Blades

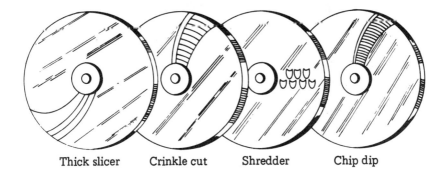

Thick slicer   Crinkle cut   Shredder   Chip dip

THICK SLICER: Use with heavy pressure for thick slices.

CRINKLE CUT: Use for soft vegetables, potatoes and cheese.

SHREDDER DISK: Use for soft cheeses and soft vegetables.

CHIP DIP: Use to slice soft vegetables for dipping.

Funnel

The FUNNEL that I designed is made of FDA-approved Lexan, and the plunger of FDA-approved polystyrene. There is a lifetime warranty and the funnel is dishwasher safe.

The funnel allows dry ingredients and liquids to be poured into the bowl without spills while the machine is on. This assures a lighter batter. You can pour in liquids, such as oil for mayonnaise or pesto, without getting a feedback.

The funnel allows larger quantities of food to be fed in at a time. With the use of the plunger, whole carrots, bananas, cucumbers, etc. can be packed into the processor tube without first cutting them.

Appetizers

Anchovy and Garlic Dip

4 cloves garlic
½ bunch parsley
2 ounces pine nuts
4 ounces anchovies
¾ cup olive oil
¼ cup red wine vinegar
¼ teaspoon Tellicherry pepper

Insert STEEL BLADE. Using the on/off method, mince together the garlic, parsley and pine nuts. Add the anchovies and continue to use the on/off method until quite smooth. Add the oil, vinegar and pepper. Process until well mixed. Chill.

Yields 2 cups.

Green Chile Cheese Dip

4 ounces green chilies
1 pimiento
8 ounces sour cream
8 ounces cream cheese

Slit the chilies and remove the seeds.

Insert STEEL BLADE. Using the on/off method, mince together the chilies and pimiento. Add the sour cream. Process until well mixed. Break up the cream cheese and add to the mixture, processing until smooth.

If the dip is too thick, add a small amount of light cream. Chill.

Yields 3 cups.

Guacamole Dip

1 ripe avocado
1 clove garlic
Juice of 1 lemon
Salt and pepper to taste
Onion, cayenne or dried red pepper flakes (optional)

Peel the avocado and remove the pit.

Insert STEEL BLADE. Using the on/off method, chop together the avocado and garlic. Add the lemon juice and seasonings. Process until smooth.

Yields ½ cup.

Curry Dip

1 scallion
1 clove garlic
4 tablespoons butter
1 slice ginger root (the size of a quarter)
1 small apple, peeled and cored
2 teaspoons curry powder
2 tablespoons flour
1 teaspoon salt
1 teaspoon sugar
2 cups milk
¼ cup lemon juice

Insert STEEL BLADE. Using the on/off method, mince together the scallion and garlic.

Melt the butter in a skillet, add the scallion and garlic and sauté until golden.

Keep STEEL BLADE in place. Using the on/off method, mince together the ginger root and apple. Insert FUNNEL and, with the motor on, add the curry powder, flour, salt, sugar and milk.

Add all ingredients except lemon juice to a saucepan and cook over medium heat, stirring constantly, until sauce begins to thicken. Reduce heat, cover and cook for 30 minutes. Remove from heat and add the lemon juice.

Yields 2 cups

Thai Chile Dip

1 small green apple
1 green chile
1 small lime
2 teaspoons brown sugar
2 anchovies
½ teaspoon salt
¼ teaspoon red pepper flakes
2 scallions

Peel the apple if waxed. Core.

Slit the chile and remove the seeds.

Zest the lime and juice it.

Insert STEEL BLADE. Using the on/off method, finely grate the lime rind with the sugar. Add the apple, green chile and anchovies, and continue to use the on/off method until well mixed. Add the lime juice, salt and red pepper flakes, and continue to use the on/off method until well mixed. Pour into a small dish.

Insert SLICING DISK. Using light pressure, slice the scallions. Sprinkle over the dip. Chill.

Yields ½ cup.

Shrimp Dip

1 small onion
1/3 cup American cheese, shredded
5 ounces cooked shrimp
½ cup mayonnaise
3 tablespoons milk
1 teaspoon Worcestershire sauce
Dash of hot pepper sauce

Insert STEEL BLADE. Using the on/off method, mince the onion. Add the cheese and shrimp. Process until smooth. Add the mayonnaise, milk, Worcestershire and hot pepper sauce. Process until smooth. Chill.

Yields 1½ cups.

Clam Dip

1 small onion
4 sprigs parsley
1 clove garlic
6 ounces clams
8 ounces cream cheese
3 tablespoons milk
1 tablespoon lemon juice
2 teaspoons horseradish
1 teaspoon salt
½ teaspoon Tellicherry pepper

Insert STEEL BLADE. Using the on/off method, mince together the onion, parsley and garlic. Add the clams and continue the on/off method until they are minced.

Break up the cream cheese and add to the clam mixture. Continue to use the on/off method until smooth. Add the remaining ingredients. Process until smooth. Chill.

Yields 2 cups

Liverwurst Pâté

3 ounces liverwurst
3 ounces cream cheese
1 tablespoon yogurt
¼ teaspoon salt
1/8 teaspoon Tellicherry pepper
Toast rounds or crackers

Preheat broiler.

Insert STEEL BLADE. Using the on/off method, blend together the liverwurst and cream cheese. Process until smooth. Add the yogurt, salt and pepper. Give the blade another turn or two.

Spread the pâté on the crackers or toast rounds. Place under the broiler 1 or 2 minutes, until bubbly.

Yields 30 canapes.

Poor Man's Caviar

1 pound eggplant
1 small onion
2 teaspoons vegetable oil
½ teaspoon vinegar
Black olives or fresh dill
½ teaspoon salt
Crackers or toast

Preheat oven to 425°.

Bake the eggplant for 20 to 25 minutes, or until tender. Scrape the pulp from the skin and discard the skin.

Insert STEEL BLADE. Using the on/off method, chop the onion. Add the eggplant and continue to use the on/off method until smooth. Add the remaining ingredients and blend. Chill.

Serve on crackers or toast and garnish with black olives or dill.

Yields 1 cup.

Meatballs

1 small onion
1 clove garlic
3 sprigs parsley
6 leaves fresh or ½ teaspoon dried basil
3 slices bread
1 pound ground chuck
1 teaspoon Tellicherry pepper
1 egg
2 tablespoons soy sauce
Butter for browning

Insert STEEL BLADE. Using the on/off method, mince together the onion, garlic, parsley, basil and bread. Add the meat and pepper. Mix well. Add the egg and soy sauce. Give the blade another turn or two.

Form mixture into 1-inch meatballs.

Heat enough butter to cover the surface of a skillet. Add the meatballs and brown on all sides. Shake the pan frequently to brown evenly. When browned, cover and cook for 10 minutes over medium heat.

Yields 40 balls.

Nachos

3 ounces Cheddar cheese
1 can (3½ ounces) jalapeño chili peppers
6 corn tortillas
1 tablespoon oil
Garlic salt
1 cup refried beans

Preheat oven to 350°.

Insert SHREDDING DISK. Shred the cheese. Set aside.

Insert SLICING DISK. Using light pressure, slice the jalapeño peppers. Remove seeds and set peppers aside.

Cut the tortillas into quarters.

Heat the oil in a skillet. Sauté a few tortillas at a time, turning constantly until they are crisp and golden brown. Drain and sprinkle with garlic salt. Spread each chip with a thin layer of beans, sprinkle with cheese and top with a slice of pepper. Place on a baking sheet and bake about 5 minutes or until the cheese melts. Serve immediately.

Yields 24 nachos.

Blue Cheese or Roquefort Dip

1 cup creamed cottage cheese
½ cup mayonnaise
4 ounces Roquefort or blue cheese, broken up

Insert PLASTIC BLADE. Process all ingredients together until smooth. Chill.

Yields 1¾ cups.

Stuffed Mushrooms

Choose mushrooms with perfect caps. Wipe clean and remove stems.

Sausage Stuffing

Mushroom stems
2 scallions
4 tablespoons butter
½ pound bulk pork sausage
3 tablespoons seasoned bread crumbs (see page 125)

Preheat oven to 350°.

Insert STEEL BLADE. Using the on/off method, finely chop the mushroom stems. Set aside.

Keep STEEL BLADE in place. Using the on/off method, finely chop the scallions.

Melt 2 tablespoons of the butter in a skillet. Add the scallions and sauté. Set aside.

Keep STEEL BLADE in place. Chop the sausage. Add to the skillet and brown.

Insert PLASTIC BLADE. Add the scallions, sausage, chopped mushroom stems and bread crumbs. Using the on/off method, process until well mixed. Return to the skillet and brown.

In another skillet, melt the remaining 2 tablespoons of butter and lightly brown the mushroom caps over medium heat. Place in a greased baking dish and stuff with sausage mixture. Bake for 30 minutes.

Florentine Stuffing

7 ounces fresh spinach
1/3 cup water
3 ounces cream cheese
2 slices cooked bacon
2 tablespoons butter
Nutmeg

Preheat oven to 350°.

Insert SLICING DISK. Using light pressure, slice the spinach. Bring water to a boil and add spinach. When it has wilted, remove and drain.

Insert STEEL BLADE. Using the on/off method, blend together the spinach, cream cheese and bacon. Prepare mushroom caps as in last step of Sausage Stuffing. Sprinkle with nutmeg.

Bake for 10 minutes.

South of the Border Stuffing

Mushroom stems
¼ pound lean beef
1 tablespoon chili pepper, chopped
4 tablespoons butter
2 ounces Cheddar cheese, shredded

Preheat oven to 350°.

Insert STEEL BLADE. Using the on/off method, chop together the mushroom stems and beef. Add the chili pepper and continue the on/off method until mixture is quite fine.

Melt 2 tablespoons of the butter in a skillet. Brown mixture.

*Prepare as in the last step of Sausage Stuffing. Bake for 15 minutes. Top with the shredded cheese and bake until the cheese melts.

Stuffings from Leftovers

Meat:
½ pound cooked meat
1 clove garlic
3 tablespoons seasoned bread crumbs (see page 125)
2 tablespoons butter

Chicken:
½ pound cooked chicken
1 slice ginger root (the size of a half dollar)
3 tablespoons seasoned bread crumbs
1 tablespoon dry sherry
2 tablespoons butter

Preheat oven to 350°.

Insert STEEL BLADE. Using the on/off method, process together all ingredients.

Prepare as in the last step of Sausage Stuffing. Bake for 15 minutes.

Each recipe will fill approximately 24 mushrooms (6 to 8 servings).

Hummus

1 can (15 ounces) garbanzo beans
¼ teaspoon powdered cumin
1 large clove garlic
¼ cup sesame paste (tahini)
3 tablespoons lemon juice
½ teaspoon salt
¼ teaspoon Tellicherry pepper

Drain the garbanzos. Reserve liquid.

Toast the cumin in a pan over low heat until the fragrance has been released.

Insert STEEL BLADE. Using the on/off method, mince the garlic with the cumin. Add the garbanzos and continue to use the on/off method until smooth. Add the sesame paste, lemon juice, salt and pepper. Process until smooth.

If the dip needs thinning, add the reserved liquid slowly while the motor is on. Chill.

Yields 1½ cups.

Crab and Water Chestnut Spread

1 clove garlic
2 ounces water chestnuts
2 scallions
½ pound cooked crabmeat
1 tablespoon soy sauce
¼ cup mayonnaise

Insert STEEL BLADE. Using the on/off method, mince the garlic. Add the water chestnuts and scallions, and continue to use the on/off method until finely chopped. Add the crabmeat, mayonnaise and soy sauce. Process until chunky. Chill overnight.

Yields 1½ cups.

Spinach Balls

1 pound fresh spinach
4 ounces Parmesan cheese
3 eggs
1 cup seasoned bread crumbs (see page 125)
4 tablespoons butter
¼ teaspoon nutmeg

Insert SLICING DISK. Using medium pressure, slice the spinach. Place in a saucepan, cover with water and bring to a boil. Drain. Rinse with cold water and drain again.

Insert STEEL BLADE. Using the on/off method, finely grate the Parmesan cheese. Set aside.

Keep STEEL BLADE in place. Beat the eggs until light and fluffy. Add the cheese, bread crumbs, butter and nutmeg. Mix well. Add the spinach and give the blade another turn or two.

Form into balls about the size of walnuts. Freeze.

Just before serving, preheat the oven to 350°. Remove the balls from the freezer and place on a cookie sheet. Set in the oven while still frozen. Bake 10 to 15 minutes.

Yields 40 balls.

Soups

Beet Borscht

6 small beets
4 cups water
1 teaspoon salt
1 tablespoon lemon juice
1 tablespoon sugar
1 egg
Sour cream

Cut the ends from the beets and scrub beets thoroughly. Cook whole in boiling water for 30 minutes. Drain, put in cold water and rub off the skins.

Insert SHREDDING DISK. Grate the beets. Place in a saucepan with the 4 cups water and the salt. Bring to a boil, then reduce heat and simmer for 30 minutes. Add the lemon juice and sugar. Continue to simmer for another 30 minutes.

Insert PLASTIC BLADE. Beat the egg. Insert FUNNEL and pour in the beet mixture. Mix well. Chill. Serve with sour cream.

4 servings.

Vegetable Soup

1 large onion, peeled
1 small turnip, peeled
¼ medium head cabbage
2 stalks celery
3 carrots
½ pound string beans
½ cup peas
4 tablespoons butter
8 ounces tomatoes
6 cups boiling water
2 teaspoons salt
1 teaspoon chopped parsley

Insert SLICING DISK. Using heavy pressure, slice the onion. Melt the butter in a saucepan. Sauté onion until soft but not brown.

Keep SLICING DISK in place. Using heavy pressure, slice the remaining vegetables, except the peas. Add the boiling water, salt, parsley and peas and boil until all vegetables are tender.

4-6 servings.

Vegetable Soup With Beef

2 pounds beef (plus shin bone, if available)
8 cups cold water
2 teaspoons salt

Cut meat into small cubes. Put the beef, bone, salt and water into a large stockpot. Cover and simmer for 4 hours.

Prepare the VEGETABLE SOUP as above, substituting beef stock for water. Add to stockpot and cook vegetables until tender.

Cream of Vegetable Soup

4 cups scalded milk
4 tablespoons melted butter
1 tablespoon flour

Prepare the VEGETABLE SOUP as above, using 4 cups of boiling water instead of 6.

When vegetables are tender, insert STEEL BLADE. Puree vegetables. Add the scalded milk, melted butter and flour, and blend.

Chicken and Corn Soup

¼ pound chicken breast meat
2 egg whites
¼ cup water
½ tablespoon dry sherry
4 cups chicken broth
¼ teaspoon salt
¼ teaspoon Muntok (or white) pepper
1 cup cream-style corn
2 tablespoons vegetable oil
3 tablespoons cornstarch
2 ounces smoked ham

Insert STEEL BLADE. Using the on/off method, chop the chicken into coarse pieces. Add 1 egg white, the water and sherry, and continue to use the on/off method until chicken is minced.

Pour the broth into a saucepan. Add the salt and pepper, then bring to a boil. Add the chicken mixture and corn, and bring to a boil.

Insert PLASTIC BLADE. Add the remaining egg white, the oil and cornstarch, and process until smooth. Add to the soup and bring to a boil.

Insert STEEL BLADE. Using the on/off method, mince the ham. Garnish soup with the ham.

6 servings.

Gazpacho

2 large ripe tomatoes
1 medium cucumber
1 large green pepper
½ bunch watercress
1 small onion
1 clove garlic
1 teaspoon dried parsley
1 teaspoon dried basil
1 teaspoon dried thyme
1 teaspoon dried tarragon
1 teaspoon dried rosemary
1 tablespoon safflower oil
3 tablespoons lemon juice
1 teaspoon salt
2 cups chilled tomato juice
Watercress for garnish

Peel the tomatoes and cut into quarters.

Peel the cucumber, remove the seeds and cut into quarters.

Quarter the green pepper and remove the seeds and membranes.

Insert STEEL BLADE. Add all the ingredients except the tomato juice. Using the on/off method, process until vegetables are chopped. With the motor on, add the tomato juice. Pour mixture into a bowl and chill thoroughly. Decorate with watercress.

4 servings.

Cold Cucumber Soup

2 cucumbers
6 to 8 sprigs parsley
2 scallions, white part only
4 cups buttermilk
2 cups sour cream
2 tablespoons lemon juice
1 teaspoon salt
Thin cucumber slices
Dill sprigs

Peel the cucumbers and remove the seeds with a teaspoon.

Insert STEEL BLADE. Using the on/off method, finely chop together the parsley and scallions. Add the cucumbers and mince. With the motor on, add 1 cup of the buttermilk and puree. Add the sour cream, lemon juice, salt and the remaining 3 cups of buttermilk. Process until smooth. Keep the motor on or the liquid will ooze out. As soon as you turn off the motor, remove the bowl from the base. Do not remove the lid. This will allow the blade to drop down, forming a short-lived vacuum.

Pour into a serving bowl, cover and refrigerate. Garnish with thin slices of cucumber and fresh dill sprigs.

6-8 servings.

French Onion Soup

6 large onions
3 tablespoons butter
4 cups beef broth
3 tablespoons dry sherry
1 teaspoon salt
½ teaspoon Tellicherry pepper
2 ounces Parmesan cheese
6 to 8 ¼-inch-thick slices French bread

Preheat oven to 375°.

Insert SLICING DISK. Using light pressure, slice the onions.

Melt the butter in a heavy pan and sauté the onions until tender and slightly browned, stirring constantly. Add the broth, sherry, salt and pepper. Bring to a boil. Boil 2 or 3 minutes.

Insert STEEL BLADE. Using the on/off method, grate the Parmesan cheese.

Pour soup into individual ovenproof bowls. Top each with a slice of French bread and sprinkle with grated cheese. Bake soup for 10 minutes, or until cheese has crusted.

6-8 servings.

Peanut Butter Soup

1 small onion
2 stalks celery
4 tablespoons butter
3 tablespoons flour
4 cups chicken broth
2 cups peanuts
1 tablespoon lemon juice
1 teaspoon salt (if unsalted peanuts are used)

Insert STEEL BLADE. Using the on/off method, mince together the onion and celery.

Melt the butter in a large saucepan. Sauté the onion and celery for about 5 minutes, but do not brown. Add the flour, mixing well. Add the chicken broth and bring to a boil. Reduce heat and simmer for 30 minutes. Strain. Return to saucepan. Keep warm over low heat.

Keep STEEL BLADE in place. Using the on/off method, chop the peanuts. Reserve ½ cup chopped nuts for garnish. Continue to process nuts until smooth and creamy. Add the lemon juice and salt. Give the blade another turn or two. Blend into the soup. Garnish with reserved chopped nuts.

6-8 servings.

Pea Soup

2 cups dried split peas
8 cups cold water
1 small onion
1 stalk celery
1 ham bone or 1 pound smoked ham or bacon
1 teaspoon salt
½ teaspoon black pepper
Croutons

Soak the peas overnight in water to cover. Drain.

Insert STEEL BLADE. Using the on/off method, finely chop together the onion, celery and ham or bacon (if used).

Place the peas, water, onion, celery, minced ham or bacon, or the ham bone, salt and pepper in a large stockpot. Cover and bring to a rolling boil. Reduce heat and simmer for 3 hours or until peas are tender.

Insert STEEL BLADE and FUNNEL. With the motor on, puree 1/3 of the soup at a time. Garnish with croutons.

8 servings.

Cheese Soup

2 carrots
2 stalks celery
1 large onion
2 tablespoons butter
3 cups chicken broth
2 teaspoons paprika
12 ounces Cheddar cheese
¼ cup flour
1 teaspoon salt
1½ cups half and half
½ teaspoon Worcestershire sauce
¼ teaspoon Muntok (or white) pepper

Insert STEEL BLADE. Using the on/off method, chop the carrots into large pieces. Add the celery and onion and continue to use the on/off method for 4 or 5 more turns.

Melt the butter in a stockpot. Add the chopped vegetables and cook for 5 minutes over medium heat. Add chicken broth and paprika and bring to a boil. Reduce heat, cover and simmer for 10 minutes.

Insert SHREDDING DISK. Shred the cheese. Add to the stockpot and stir until melted.

Insert PLASTIC BLADE. Add the flour and salt. With the motor on, slowly add the half and half. Process until well blended. Add to the stockpot. Cook and stir slightly until soup thickens. Add the Worcestershire and pepper.

Marvelous as a vegetable sauce, too.

4 servings.

Cream of Cauliflower Soup

1 pound cauliflower, cleaned and trimmed
3 large potatoes, peeled and quartered
4 cups milk
1 teaspoon salt
3 slices stale white bread
2 tablespoons butter
4 sprigs parsley
Oil or butter for sautéeing croutons

Cook cauliflower in boiling salted water until barely tender, about 8 minutes. Drain.

In saucepan, combine the cauliflower, potatoes, 2 cups of the milk and the salt, and bring to a boil. Cover and simmer for 20 minutes. Strain, reserving the liquid.

While vegetables are simmering, prepare the croutons. Trim the crust from the bread. Cut bread into ½-inch cubes. Fry until golden brown in butter or oil. Another way to prepare croutons is to butter the bread and cut into cubes. Crisp in a hot (450°) oven.

Insert STEEL BLADE. Using the on/off method, puree the vegetables. With the motor on, add the reserved liquid. Return to saucepan and bring to a boil. Add the remaining 2 cups milk. Remove from heat. Stir in the butter until melted.

Keep STEEL BLADE. Using the on/off method, chop the parsley.

Place the croutons in the bottom of each soup bowl and pour the soup over them. Garnish with the chopped parsley.

4 servings.

Black Bean Soup

2 cups dried black beans
1 teaspoon salt
1 teaspoon red pepper flakes
½ teaspoon pepper
1 ham bone, or 1 pound smoked ham or bacon
1 large onion
2 cloves garlic
¼ cup sweet sherry
2 tablespoons lemon juice
Minced onions or lemon slices

Soak the beans in water overnight. Drain.

Place the beans and water, salt, red pepper flakes, pepper and ham bone (if used) in a large stock pot. Bring to a boil.

Insert STEEL BLADE. Using the on/off method, mince together the onion, garlic and ham or bacon (if used). Add to the beans. Reduce the heat and simmer for 3 hours, until beans are tender. Check the water level after an hour—liquid should remain approximately ½ inch above the beans. Remove from heat. Add the sherry and lemon juice.

Insert STEEL BLADE and FUNNEL. Puree 1/3 of the beans at a time. Reheat and garnish with minced onions or lemon slices.

This soup can also be served over cooked rice.

6-8 servings.

Tomato Soup

1 pound fresh tomatoes, or 1 large can tomatoes
2 cups water
4 whole cloves
1 scallion, white part only, sliced
2 teaspoons sugar
1 teaspoon salt
2 tablespoons butter
2 tablespoons flour

Cut the tomatoes into quarters.

Cook the first 6 ingredients in a stockpot for 20 minutes over medium heat.

Insert STEEL BLADE. Using the on/off method, cut the butter into the flour. With the motor on, add the tomato mixture and process until smooth.

4-6 servings.

Cream of Tomato Soup

Prepare as above, adding 2 cups scalded milk after the tomato mixture has been processed.

Entrees

Shepherd's Pie

1 small onion
½ pound cooked beef
¼ teaspoon salt
1/8 teaspoon Tellicherry pepper
2 tablespoons beef gravy to moisten
1 cup mashed potatoes

Preheat oven to 425°.

Insert STEEL BLADE. Using the on/off method, chop the onion into large pieces. Add the beef, salt and pepper, and continue to use the on/off method until beef is chunky. Add the gravy and give the blade another turn or two.

Place in a greased baking dish and top with the mashed potatoes. Bake for 15 minutes, or until the potatoes are light brown.

2 servings.

Lamb Curry

1½ pounds lean lamb
2 tablespoons vegetable oil
1 tablespoon curry powder (or more, if desired)
3 cloves garlic
2 large onions
1 tomato
1 medium tart apple, peeled and cored
¼ cup raisins
2 cups chicken broth
Italian parsley

Trim the lamb and shape to fit the tube. Place meat in the freezer for 45 minutes, or just long enough to give it body. Remove.

Insert SLICING DISK. Using heavy pressure, slice the lamb.

Heat the oil in a skillet and sauté the sliced lamb until browned. Add the curry powder, stirring until meat is covered. Remove lamb and set aside.

Insert STEEL BLADE. Using the on/off method, mince the garlic. Add to the skillet and cook briefly over low heat.

Insert SLICING DISK. Cut the onions and tomatoes in half. Using heavy pressure, slice. Add to the garlic and cook until soft.

Insert STEEL BLADE. Using the on/off method, chop the apple into chunks. Add the apple, raisins, and 1 cup of the chicken broth to the skillet. Bring to a boil. Add the remaining cup of broth. Return to a boil. Reduce the heat, cover and simmer until lamb is tender, about 2 hours.

Insert STEEL BLADE. Using the on/off method, mince the Italian parsley. Sprinkle on the curry. Serve the curry with chutney or rice.

6 servings.

Variations

Beef Curry: Substitute beef for lamb.
Chicken Curry: Substitute chicken for lamb. Omit the apple and raisins.
Shrimp curry: Use shrimp in place of lamb. Omit garlic, 1 onion, tomato and raisins. Add another apple and 1 tablespoon lemon juice.

Beef Casserole

1½ pounds sirloin or flank steak
1/3 cup flour
1 pound potatoes, peeled
¼ medium head cabbage
4 carrots
4 stalks celery
1 small onion
1 teaspoon dried basil
1 teaspoon dried marjoram
1 cup beef bouillon
1 teaspoon salt
½ teaspoon Tellicherry pepper
½ cup sherry
3 tomatoes

Trim the fat from the beef. Shape to fit the tube. Place in the freezer for 30 to 45 minutes, or just long enough to give the meat body. Remove.

Preheat oven to 350°.

Insert SLICING DISK. Using heavy pressure, slice the beef. Coat all sides of the meat with flour. Place in a casserole dish.

Keep SLICING DISK in place. Using light pressure, slice the potatoes. Using heavy pressure, slice the cabbage, carrots and celery. Place in the greased casserole.

Insert STEEL BLADE. Using the on/off method, chop the onion with the basil and marjoram. With the motor on, add the bouillon, salt, pepper and sherry. Pour mixture into the casserole.

Insert SLICING DISK. Using heavy pressure, slice the tomatoes. Arrange on top of the casserole. Bake for 45 minutes.

6 servings.

Meat Loaf with Tomato Sauce

1½ pounds lean beef, cut into cubes
2 ounces Cheddar cheese
1 small onion
4 sprigs parsley
6 saltine crackers
2 tablespoons Worcestershire sauce
1 egg
1 teaspoon salt
½ teaspoon Tellicherry pepper
1 cup tomato sauce

Preheat oven to 350°.

Insert STEEL BLADE. Using the on/off method, coarsely chop ½ pound of meat at a time. Set aside.

Insert SHREDDING DISK. Shred the cheese. Set aside.

Insert STEEL BLADE. Using the on/off method, coarsely chop together the onion and parsley. Add the saltines and continue to use the on/off method until crumbs are made. Add the meat, cheese, Worcestershire, egg, salt, pepper and ½ cup of the tomato sauce. Continue to use the on/off method until well mixed.

Form a loaf and place in a greased loaf pan (9 by 5 by 3 inches). Pour the remaining ½ cup tomato sauce over the top. Bake for 1 hour.

4 servings.

Variations

Use 1 pound beef, ¼ pound pork and ¼ pound veal.

For plain meat loaf without the tomato sauce, use ½ cup milk in place of the tomato sauce.

Sorrento-Style Veal

12 veal cutlets
8 ounces mozzarella cheese
½ pound cooked ham
½ pound mushrooms
2 ounces Parmesan cheese
½ pound ripe tomatoes
4 sprigs Italian parsley
1 teaspoon dried oregano
1 cup dry white wine
4 tablespoons butter
¼ cup olive oil
1 teaspoon salt
½ teaspoon Tellicherry pepper

Pound the cutlets until very thin.

Preheat oven to 425°.

Insert SLICING DISK. Using heavy pressure, slice the mozzarella cheese, ham and mushrooms. Set aside.

Insert STEEL BLADE. Using the on/off method, grate the Parmesan cheese. Set aside.

Keep the STEEL BLADE in place. Using the on/off method, chop together the tomatoes and parlsey. Add the oregano and with the motor on, add the wine.

Pour into a saucepan, cover and cook over high heat for 10 minutes. The sauce should be very thick.

Heat the butter and oil in a skillet. Sauté the cutlets on both sides. Sprinkle with salt and pepper.

In a greased baking dish, layer the veal, ham, mushrooms, mozzarella and tomato sauce. Sprinkle with Parmesan cheese. Bake for about 15 minutes, until cheese melts.

4-6 servings.

Pork Chops and Apricots

4 thick pork chops
½ teaspoon dried marjoram
½ teaspoon dried oregano
½ teaspoon dried basil
½ teaspoon dried dill
4 sprigs parsley
8 ounces canned apricot halves
¼ pound mushrooms
1 small onion
1 tablespoon butter
1½ cups cream of mushroom soup or 1 can cream of mushroom soup, diluted
¼ cup dry white wine

Preheat oven to 350°.

Place the chops in a large shallow baking dish that has been greased.

Insert STEEL BLADE. Using the on/off method, mince together all the herbs. Sprinkle over the pork chops.

Drain the apricots, reserving ½ cup of the liquid. Place two apricot halves on each pork chop, skin side up.

Insert SLICING DISK. Using heavy pressure, slice the mushrooms and onion.

Melt the butter in a skillet and sauté the onion and mushrooms until soft.

Insert PLASTIC BLADE. Add the mushroom soup and, with the motor on, add the wine and reserved apricot liquid. Process until well mixed. Add the cooked onions and mushrooms, mixing well. Pour over the chops. Bake for 1 hour.

4 servings.

Variations

Substitute peaches, plums or apples for the apricots.

Welsh Rarebit

12 ounces Cheddar cheese
1 tablespoon butter
1 teaspoon cornstarch
½ teaspoon dry mustard
¼ teaspoon salt
1/8 teaspoon cayenne
¾ cup light cream
1 egg
4 slices toast

Insert SHREDDING DISK. Shred the cheese. Set aside.

Insert PLASTIC BLADE. Using the on/off method, soften the butter. Add the cornstarch, mustard, salt and cayenne. With the motor on, add the cream.

Pour into a saucepan. Cook over medium heat, stirring constantly, for 2 minutes. Add the cheese and continue to cook until all the cheese has melted.

Keep PLASTIC BLADE in place. Beat the egg. Insert FUNNEL and, with the motor on, pour in the cheese mixture. Process until smooth and creamy. Serve on toast.

4 servings.

Variation

Substitute ¾ cup beer for the light cream and cornstarch.

Baked Chicken Supreme

1 large whole chicken breast, split
1 clove garlic
¾ cup sour cream
1 tablespoon lemon juice
1 teaspoon paprika
½ teaspoon salt
¼ teaspoon Tellicherry pepper
1/3 cup white wine
1 teaspoon Worcestershire sauce
¾ cup bread crumbs
Parsley

Preheat oven to 350°.

Wash the chicken breast and place in a greased baking dish.

Insert STEEL BLADE. Using the on/off method, finely chop the garlic.

Insert PLASTIC BLADE. Add the sour cream, lemon juice, paprika, salt and pepper. Process until smooth.

Cover the chicken with the sour cream mixture. Sprinkle the wine and Worcestershire over the sour cream sauce. Sprinkle on the bread crumbs. Bake for 1 hour, or until chicken is crisp and tender. Garnish with parsley.

2 servings.

Chicken Croquettes

2 scallions
4 sprigs parsley
½ pound cooked chicken
½ cup bread crumbs
½ cup light cream
1 teaspoon butter
¼ teaspoon celery salt
1/8 teaspoon Tellicherry pepper
1 egg white
¼ cup duxelles (optional—see potpourri)
1 cup cracker crumbs
Oil for frying

Insert STEEL BLADE. Using the on/off method, chop together the scallions and parsley.

Insert SLICING DISK. Using heavy pressure, slice the chicken.

Insert PLASTIC BLADE. With the motor on, add the bread crumbs, cream, butter, celery salt, pepper, duxelles, and egg white. Give the blade another turn or two. Turn mixture into a bowl and chill for 30 minutes.

To form croquettes, take about 1 tablespoon of the mixture, make a small ball and roll between your palms. Then roll on a board to get the desired length and size. Roll in cracker crumbs and deep fry in oil preheated to 350°. Fry until golden brown, about 1 minute.

4 servings.

Variations

Croquettes can be made from any leftover meat such as ham, veal or turkey. Follow the above recipe if turkey is used.

Ham: 2 cups scalded milk and 2 rounded teaspoons cornstarch in place of light cream and bread crumbs.

Veal: Use 1 egg yolk and 1 cup thick white sauce in place of the egg white, light cream and bread crumbs.

Chicken Pot Pie

One 3½ pound chicken
1 small onion
1 carrot
1 stalk celery
6 scallions
1 teaspoon salt
¼ teaspoon Muntok (or white) pepper
8 mushrooms
6 slices bacon
4 tablespoons flour
2 tablespoons lemon juice
Pastry for 9-inch 1-crust pie (see page 108)
3 tablespoons butter

Wash the chicken and place in a stockpot with 6 cups of water. Bring to a boil.

Insert STEEL BLADE. Using the on/off method, finely chop together the onion, carrot, celery and scallions. Add to the stockpot. Add salt and pepper. Reduce heat, cover and simmer for 40 minutes. Remove the chicken. Reserve the broth and vegetables. Skin and remove meat from the bones. Cool.

Preheat oven to 450°.

Insert SLICING DISK. Using heavy pressure, slice the chicken. Remove to a casserole dish. Slice the mushrooms.

Fry bacon until crisp. Drain. Sauté the mushrooms in the bacon drippings. Drain. Add to chicken.

Insert STEEL BLADE. Using the on/off method, crumble the bacon. Add to the chicken and mushrooms.

Keep STEEL BLADE in place. Pour in the flour. Insert FUNNEL and, with motor on, add the bacon drippings. Process until a paste is made. Add 1½ cups of reserved chicken broth. Pour into skillet. Simmer over medium heat, stirring frequently, for 10 minutes. Stir in the lemon juice, then pour mixture over the chicken.

Cover the casserole with pie crust and dot with the butter. Make several slits in the crust. Bake for 10 minutes. Reduce heat to 350° and bake 20 minutes longer or until golden brown.

4-6 servings.

Stuffed Snapper

½ cup almonds
2 slices bread
6 mushrooms
1 scallion
4 sprigs parsley
½ pound cooked shrimp
1 egg
½ teaspoon salt
½ teaspoon Muntok (or white) pepper
2-pound snapper, cut in half, or 2 pounds snapper fillets.

Preheat oven to 375°.

Insert STEEL BLADE. Using the on/off method, coarsely chop together the almonds and bread. Add the mushrooms, scallion, parsley and shrimp, and continue to use the on/off method until shrimp is chopped into large chunks. Add the egg, salt and pepper, and process until chunky.

Stuff the snapper. If fillets are used, make a sandwich of two fillets and stuffing. Place in buttered baking dish. Bake until fish is flaky, about 1 hour.

4 servings.

Maryland Crabs

3 tablespoons butter
1 tablespoon flour
½ cup milk
2 eggs
2 tablespoons mayonnaise
2 teaspoons Worcestershire sauce
1 teaspoon dry mustard
1 teaspoon salt
¼ teaspoon cayenne
1 pound fresh crabmeat
6 teaspoons bread crumbs

Preheat oven to 500°.

Insert STEEL BLADE. Process 1 tablespoon of the butter with the flour. Insert FUNNEL and, with the motor on, add the milk, eggs, mayonnaise, Worcestershire sauce, mustard, salt and cayenne. Process until well mixed. Add the crabmeat and give the blade another turn or two.

Spoon the mixture into greased ramekins. Sprinkle with bread crumbs. Dot with the remaining 2 tablespoons of butter. Bake until golden brown, about 15 minutes.

6 servings.

Crab or Lobster Quiche

2 eggs
¼ pound cooked crabmeat or lobster
½ cup heavy cream
1 tablespoon lemon juice
1 tablespoon sherry
½ teaspoon salt
½ teaspoon dried thyme
9-inch partially baked Quiche Pastry Shell (see page 124)
Pinch of nutmeg
Pinch of paprika

Preheat oven to 375°.

Insert STEEL BLADE. Beat the eggs lightly. Add the crabmeat or lobster and give the blade another turn or two. Add the cream, lemon juice, sherry, salt and thyme. Blend lightly.

Pour the mixture into the baked quiche shell. Sprinkle with nutmeg and paprika. Bake for 20 minutes, or until a knife inserted in the filling comes out clean. Serve at room temperature.

4 servings.

Shrimp de Jonghe

2 cloves garlic
1 scallion
4 sprigs parsley
4 sprigs chervil
4 sprigs tarragon
1 teaspoon salt
½ teaspoon Muntok (or white) pepper
½ cup butter
¾ cup bread crumbs
½ cup dry sherry
2 pounds cooked shrimp

Preheat oven to 450°.

Insert STEEL BLADE. Using the on/off method, mince together the garlic, scallion, parsley, chervil and tarragon. Add the salt and pepper. With the motor on, add the butter, bread crumbs and sherry. Process until well mixed.

Arrange the shrimp in a buttered baking dish. Top with the herb mixture. Bake for 5 minutes, or until the topping is bubbly.

4 servings.

Mussels with Garlic and Herb Sauce

3 pounds mussels
2 cloves garlic
6 sprigs parsley
6 chives
6 sprigs basil
4 mushrooms
½ cup olive oil
1 cup dry white wine
½ teaspoon Muntok (or white) pepper
2 teaspoons lemon juice
1 teaspoon salt

Scrub the mussels, rinsing several times in cold water. Drain. Cook in a large saucepan over medium heat. When all of the mussels are open, drain. Strain and reserve the liquid. Remove half the shell from each mussel.

Insert STEEL BLADE. Using the on/off method, mince the garlic. Add the parsley, chives, basil and mushrooms, and continue to use the on/off method until finely chopped.

In the saucepan, bring the oil and the chopped herbs to a boil. Add the wine and 1 cup of the reserved liquid, and continue to boil until mixture thickens. Stir frequently. Add the pepper and the mussels. Heat thoroughly. Just before serving, add the lemon juice and salt.

6 servings.

Shrimp and Artichoke Casserole

5 scallions
6 sprigs parsley
4 chives, or 2 tablespoons dried chives
5 basil leaves or ½ tablespoon dried basil
6 sprigs dill, or ½ tablespoon dried dill
4 ounces Cheddar cheese
1 can (20 ounces) artichoke hearts, drained
1 pound cooked shrimp
1 cup tomato juice
Juice of ½ lemon
2 tablespoons olive oil
2 tablespoons dry sherry
1 teaspoon salt
½ teaspoon Muntok (or white) pepper
2 ounces Parmesan cheese

Preheat oven to 350°.

Insert STEEL BLADE. Using the on/off method, chop together the scallions, parsley, chives, basil and dill.

Insert SHREDDING DISK. Shred the Cheddar cheese.

Line a 2-quart greased casserole with the artichoke hearts. Sprinkle the herb-cheese mixture over the top. Layer the shrimp over the herb-cheese mixture.

Insert PLASTIC BLADE. Mix together the tomato and lemon juices. Add the oil, sherry, salt and pepper, mixing well. Pour over the shrimp.

Insert STEEL BLADE. Using the on/off method, finely grate the Parmesan cheese. Sprinkle over the casserole. Bake until bubbly, about 30 minutes.

4 servings.

Crab and Lobster Mousse

Stock:
1 small onion
1 carrot
1 stalk celery
1 cup clam juice
1 tablespoon lemon juice
1 teaspoon salt
½ teaspoon Muntok (or white) pepper
½ teaspoon dried marjoram
½ teaspoon dried tarragon
2 sprigs parsley

3 tablespoons unflavored gelatin
¼ cup dry vermouth
2 cups cooked crabmeat
1 cup cooked lobster
3 tablespoons cognac
2 cups heavy cream

To make stock, insert SLICING DISK. Using light pressure, slice the onion, carrot and celery. Place in a saucepan with the remaining stock ingredients. Bring to a boil, then reduce heat and simmer for 10 minutes. Strain.

Insert PLASTIC BLADE. Add the gelatin and, with the motor on, add the vermouth. Insert FUNNEL. With motor on, add the stock. Set mixture aside.

Insert STEEL BLADE. Using the on/off method, chop together the crabmeat and lobster until pasty. Insert FUNNEL. Add the stock mixture and cognac. Process until smooth. Set mixture aside.

Keep STEEL BLADE in place. Whip the cream. Fold into the crabmeat-lobster mixture. Pour into a greased 6-cup mold. Refrigerate 2 hours or more.

Unmold. Serve with toast as an appetizer or with a salad as an entree.

8 servings as an entree.

Corned or Roast Beef Hash

1 pound cooked corned or roast beef
4 medium potatoes, boiled and peeled
1 small onion
½ green pepper
3 tablespoons butter
Salt and pepper to taste
¼ cup boiling water

Cut the meat into cubes.

Cut the potatoes, onion and green pepper in half.

Insert STEEL BLADE. Using the on/off method, chop the onion and green pepper into large pieces. Add the meat and continue to use the on/off method until meat and vegetables are coarsely chopped. Add the potatoes and continue to use the on/off method until hash consistency has been reached.

Melt the butter in skillet. Add hash to skillet. Add salt, pepper and the boiling water. Cook over low heat for about 40 minutes or until a crust forms on the bottom. Fold in half and turn onto a hot platter.

This is also an excellent stuffing for green peppers.

4 servings.

Quenelles with Normande Sauce

1 large shallot
½ pound pike or other white fish fillets
1 egg white
1 cup heavy cream
½ teaspoon salt
¼ cup dry white wine

Normande Sauce:
½ cup butter
2 mushrooms
4 egg yolks
2 tablespoons poaching liquid
¼ cup cream
1 teaspooon lemon juice
¼ teaspoon salt
1/8 teaspoon cayenne
1 tablespoon brandy or cognac

Insert STEEL BLADE. Using the on/off method, mince the shallot. Set aside.

Keep STEEL BLADE in place. Using the on/off method, mince the fish. Add the egg white, cream and salt. Process until thick and creamy.

Pour the wine into a large skillet and add enough water to bring the liquid up 1 inch. Bring to a boil. Add the shallot, then reduce heat and simmer. Gently drop a tablespoon of the fish mixture into the liquid and poach for 8 to 10 minutes, basting constantly with the liquid. Remove the quenelles with a slotted spoon. Drain on paper towels. Reserve 2 tablespoons poaching liquid for the sauce.

To make the sauce, heat the butter in a saucepan until bubbly.

Insert STEEL BLADE. Using the on/off method, chop the mushrooms. Insert FUNNEL and, with the motor on, add the egg yolks, reserved poaching liquid, cream, lemon juice, salt, cayenne, melted butter and brandy or cognac. Pour into a bain-marie or the top of a double boiler. Stir until thickened. Let sauce rest 5 minutes before serving. Spoon generously over the quenelles.

4 servings.

Omelet

4 large eggs
¼ cup milk
½ teaspoon salt
2 tablespoons butter

Insert PLASTIC BLADE. Add the eggs and, with the motor on, add the milk and salt. Process until mixed.

Melt the butter over medium heat in an omelet pan. Pour in the egg mixture. As it cooks, lift with a spatula letting the liquid run underneath until the whole omelet is creamy.

Increase the heat to high and brown the omelet slightly. Fold the omelet: Hold the pan by the handle. With a case knife, make a 2½-inch incision at the handle and one just opposite. Place a knife under the omelet near the handle and tip the pan vertically. Slip the omelet out with a knife. It will turn and fold without breaking. Turn it onto a hot platter.

2 servings.

Variations

Cheese: Add ½ cup shredded cheese of your choice to the egg mixture after it has been poured into the pan.

Jelly or jam: Add just before folding the omelet.

Spanish: Prepare this sauce before making the omelet:

Insert SLICING DISK. Using heavy pressure, slice 1 stalk celery, 1 small onion, 1 carrot, ½ each green and red pepper and 2 tomatoes . Add all but tomatoes to 1 tablespoon melted butter in a skillet and brown slightly. If necessary, add a tablespoon of water to prevent the vegetables from sticking. When vegetables are golden brown, add 1 teaspoon salt, ½ teaspoon Tellicherry pepper, the tomatoes and 1/3 cup water. Cook for 20 minutes, or until sauce thickens.

Pour sauce on one side of the omelet before folding. Pour more sauce over the folded omelet.

Eggplant Parmigiana

3½ pounds eggplant, peeled
1 tablespoon salt
8 ounces mozzarella cheese
8 ounces Parmesan cheese
½ cup Italian bread crumbs
2 eggs
1 tablespoon water
1/3 cup olive oil
Sauce:
2½ pounds fresh ripe tomatoes, peeled, or 1 can (35 ounces)
Italian plum tomatoes
4 tablespoons olive oil
3 sprigs basil
2 teaspoons dried oregano
1½ teaspoons salt
¼ teaspoon Tellicherry pepper

Insert SLICING DISK. Using heavy pressure, slice the eggplant. Place in a collander and sprinkle with the 1 tablespoon salt. Let stand for 1 hour. Wipe the slices dry with paper towels.

Keep SLICING DISK in place. Using heavy pressure, slice the mozzarella cheese. Set aside.

Insert STEEL BLADE. Using the on/off method, grate the Parmesan cheese. Set aside.

Insert PLASTIC BLADE. Blend bread crumbs with ½ cup of the grated Parmesan cheese. Place mixture on a flat dish.

Keep PLASTIC BLADE in place. Beat the eggs with the water. Pour into another flat dish.

Coat the eggplant slices with the egg mixture, then dip into the bread crumb mixture, shaking off any excess crumbs.

Heat 2 tablespoons of the 1/3 cup oil in a skillet. Fry the eggplant, a few slices at a time, until golden brown and crisp. Add more oil as needed. Drain on paper towels.

To make sauce, insert SLICING DISK. Using heavy pressure, slice the tomatoes. Heat the 4 tablespoons oil in a deep saucepan, and add the tomato slices.

Insert STEEL BLADE. Using the on/off method, mince together the basil and oregano. Add to the tomatoes. Cook over high heat until a sauce has been made. Stir in the 1½ teaspoons salt and the pepper.

Arrange a layer of eggplant in a wide, shallow baking dish. Sprinkle with Parmesan cheese, add a layer of mozzarella cheese and cover with tomato sauce. Repeat layers, ending with a layer of eggplant sprinkled with Parmesan cheese. Bake until cheese is melted, about 40 minutes.

6 servings.

Pizza

Dough:
1 package yeast
1 cup lukewarm water
3½ cups flour
1 teaspoon salt
2 tablespoons olive oil

Tomato Sauce:
1 large onion
3 tablespoons olive oil
1 clove garlic
4 cups plum tomatoes
6 ounce can tomato paste
1 tablespoon dried oregano
1 teaspoon dried basil
2 teaspoons sugar
1 teaspoon salt
¼ teaspoon pepper
1 bay leaf

To make the dough, dissolve yeast in lukewarm water.

Insert STEEL BLADE. Sift together the flour and salt into the processor bowl. With the motor on, add the yeast and water to the flour and salt. Using the on/off method, knead. Add the oil and continue to knead until a ball forms.

Remove the dough and knead slightly with your hands. Put in a greased bowl and cover with a towel. Set in a warm place and let rise until doubled, about 3 hours.

While the dough is rising, make the tomato sauce. Insert STEEL BLADE. Using the fast on/off method, chop the onion.

Heat the oil in a skillet and sauté the onion for 5 minutes, until transparent but not brown.

Keep STEEL BLADE in place. Using the on/off method, mince the garlic. Add tomatoes and tomato paste, and puree. Add the remaining ingredients except the bay leaf, and process until smooth.

Pour into the skillet and add the bay leaf. Bring to a boil, reduce heat and simmer uncovered until thickened, about 1 hour.

Preheat oven to 450°. When the dough has risen, spread it in a large well-greased pan to a thickness of ½ to ¾ inch. Pour the tomato sauce generously over the dough.

For topping, add your choice of ½ pound grated mozzarella (heavy pressure), sliced mushrooms (heavy pressure), sliced pepperoni (light pressure), sliced onion (light pressure), anchovies, green pepper (heavy pressure) or any ingredients desired.

Bake for 30 minutes. Reduce heat to 350° and bake 15 minutes longer.

4 servings.

Quiche Lorraine

½ pound bacon or ¼ pound ham
9-inch partially baked Quiche Pastry Shell (see page 124)
8 ounces Swiss cheese
3 eggs
2 cups light cream
Nutmeg

Preheat oven to 400°.

If using bacon, fry until crisp. Drain. Crumble bacon and sprinkle over the pastry shell. If using ham, insert STEEL BLADE. Chop coarsely. Sprinkle over the pastry shell.

Insert SHREDDING DISK. Grate the cheese. Sprinkle over the bacon or ham.

Insert PLASTIC BLADE. Beat the eggs slightly, then add the cream and process until smooth. Pour over the bacon and cheese. Sprinkle with nutmeg. Bake for 35 to 45 minutes or until a knife inserted in the center comes out clean. Serve at room temperature.

6 servings.

Shrimp Quiche

¼ pound cooked shrimp
1 scallion
1 egg
½ cup heavy cream
1 teaspoon dried basil
½ teaspoon salt
½ teaspoon Muntok (or white) pepper
4 ounces Cheddar cheese
9-inch partially baked Quiche Pastry Shell (see page 124)

Preheat oven to 375°.

Insert STEEL BLADE. Using the on/off method, chop together the shrimp and scallion. Add the egg and cream, and process until well mixed. Add the basil, salt and pepper. Process until mixed. Pour into the pastry shell.

Insert SHREDDING DISK. Shred the cheese, then sprinkle over the shrimp-egg mixture. Bake for 20 minutes, or until a knife inserted in the center comes out clean. Serve at room temperature.

4 servings.

Vegetables

Carrots in Orange Juice

1 bunch small carrots
2 cups water
½ cup orange juice
½ teaspoon salt
3 tablespoons butter
1 tablespoon flour
2 tablespoons grated orange rind

Insert SLICING DISK. Pack the tube horizontally with the carrots and, using heavy pressure, slice.

Place in a saucepan. Add the water, orange juice and salt. Bring to a boil. Skim. Reduce heat, cover and simmer until tender, about 1 hour. Watch carefully and shake the pan to prevent sticking. If necessary, add boiling water.

Insert PLASTIC BLADE. Process butter until smooth. With the motor on, add the flour, then add the orange rind. Stir into the carrots and cook for 2 minutes.

4 servings.

Potatoes Anna

4 medium potatoes, peeled
½ cup melted butter

Preheat oven to 450°.

Insert THIN SLICING DISK. Using light pressure, slice the potatoes.

Pour a small amount of the melted butter into an ovenproof skillet and stack the potatoes in the skillet. Cover with remaining butter. Place the skillet on the lowest rack of the oven. Bake for 1 hour, or until golden brown. It may be necessary to use a spatula to loosen the potatoes around the edges and bottom of the skillet before serving.

Invert the contents of the skillet onto a serving platter. Pour off the excess butter.

The potatoes can be kept warm in an oven without losing their crispness.

4 servings.

Baked Yams with Apples

3 small yams or sweet potatoes
3 large tart apples
6 tablespoons butter
½ cup light brown sugar, firmly packed
¼ cup water

Preheat oven to 475°.

Boil the yams or sweet potatoes in their skins until almost tender, about 20 minutes. Drain, let cool and peel.

Peel the apples if waxed. Core.

Insert SLICING DISK. Using medium pressure, slice the yams and apples. Arrange in a greased baking dish, dot with butter and sprinkle with brown sugar and water.

Bake for about 10 minutes until apples are tender. Baste once or twice during baking. Serve hot.

4 servings.

Onions and Sour Cream

4 large onions
1 pint sour cream
1 cup water
¼ cup lemon juice
Grated peel of ½ lemon
1 teaspoon salt
½ teaspoon Muntok (or white) pepper
½ bunch basil

Preheat oven to 350°.

Insert THIN SLICING DISK. Using light pressure, slice the onions. Arrange in a buttered baking dish.

Insert PLASTIC BLADE. Mix together the sour cream, water, lemon juice, grated peel, salt and pepper. Pour over the oinons.

Insert STEEL BLADE. Using the on/off method, chop the basil. Sprinkle over the onions. Bake for about 30 minutes, until onions are tender.

4 servings.

Plantain Chips

Oil for frying
1 unripe plantain, peeled
Salt

Pour about 3 inches of cooking oil into a skillet. Heat to 375°.

Insert THIN SLICING DISK. Using light pressure, slice the plantain into paper-thin slices.

Drop slices into the heated oil and fry for 2 or 3 minutes, or until golden brown. Fry a few at a time to prevent sticking. Drain on brown paper and sprinkle lightly with salt.

Yields 2 cups.

Baked Carrot Ring

6 medium carrots
2 eggs, separated
1 small onion
12 Ritz crackers
2 tablespoons butter, melted
¾ cup milk
½ teaspoon salt
¼ teaspoon Muntok (or white) pepper
Fresh dill or parsley

Insert SLICING DISK. Using heavy pressure, slice the carrots. (The carrots do not need to be perfect slices because they will be mashed after cooking.) Place in a saucepan, cover with water and cook over high heat for 20 minutes, or until tender.

Preheat oven to 350°.

Insert STEEL BLADE. Beat the egg whites with a pinch of salt until stiff and dry. Set aside in a large bowl.

Keep STEEL BLADE in place. Using the on/off method, mince the onion. Add the crackers and continue to use the on/off method until crumbs have been made. Add the butter and give the blade another turn or two. Insert FUNNEL. With the motor on, add the carrots, egg yolks, milk, salt and pepper. When carrots are mashed, fold mixture into the egg whites.

Pour into an 8-inch greased ring mold. Place in a 1-inch water bath. Bake for 45 minutes, or until the mixture pulls away from the sides and a knife inserted in the center comes out clean.

Unmold and garnish with fresh dill or parsley. Fill the center with peas or any green vegetable. A light lemon sauce also complements the dish.

Lemon Sauce

3 tablespoons butter
1 tablespoon lemon juice
½ teaspoon cornstarch

Melt the butter. Stir in the lemon juice and cornstarch. Simmer for 30 to 45 seconds.

8 servings.

Potato and Cheese Pie

Pastry for 9-inch 1-crust pie (see page 108)
1½ cups cottage cheese
½ cup sour cream
4 large potatoes, peeled, boiled and still warm
½ teaspoon salt
2 tablespoons milk
1 tablespoon butter

Preheat oven to 350°.

Line a pie plate with the pie crust pastry.

Insert STEEL BLADE. Process the cottage cheese until smooth. Add the sour cream and warm potatoes. Process until mixed. Add the salt and give the blade another turn or two.

Fill the pie crust with the potato mixture, brush the top with milk and dot with butter. Bake until golden, for about 45 minutes. Serve hot or cold.

4 servings.

Potato Gnocchi

2 ounces Parmesan cheese
4 pounds potatoes, peeled, boiled and still warm
1½ cups flour
8 cups water
2 tablespoons salt
3 cups tomato sauce

Insert STEEL BLADE. Using the on/off method, grate the cheese. Set aside.

Keep STEEL BLADE in place. Using the on/off method, mash the potatoes. Add the flour and process until well mixed.

Empty out onto a floured board and roll into ropes about as thick as a pen and about 2 inches long. Press each piece lightly with a fork.

Bring the water and salt to a boil in a large pan. Place about 20 gnocchi in the boiling water. The gnocchi will float to the top when done. Remove with a slotted spoon or strainer. Repeat until all the gnocchi are cooked.

Heat the tomato sauce, then pour it over the gnocchi. Sprinkle with the cheese.

4 servings.

Curried Vegetables

½ pound potatoes, peeled
½ pound carrots
1 small turnip, peeled
1 stalk celery
1 small zucchini
1 small red pepper
¼ pound peas

Sauce:
2 tablespoons flour
1 tablespoon curry powder
1 cup milk
2 tablespoons melted butter

Insert SLICING DISK. Using heavy pressure, slice all the vegetables except the peas. Place all vegetables in a saucepan and bring to a boil. Reduce heat to medium and cook for 20 minutes.

To make sauce, insert STEEL BLADE. Add the flour and curry powder. With the motor on, add the milk and melted butter. Process until smooth. Place in a saucepan and bring to a boil. Boil for 2 minutes, stirring constantly.

Drain the vegetables. Cover with the sauce.

6 servings.

Petits Pois à la Française

1 small head Boston or bibb lettuce
4 small white onions
3 tablespoons butter
1 package (10 ounces) frozen petite peas
¼ cup chicken broth
4 sprigs parsley
½ teaspoon salt
¼ teaspoon Tellicherry pepper
1 teaspoon flour

Insert THIN SLICING DISK. Using light pressure, slice the lettuce and onions.

Melt 2 tablespoons of the butter in a saucepan. Add the peas, lettuce, onions, chicken broth, parsley, salt and pepper. Cover and cook gently over low heat for 45 minutes to 1 hour.

Insert PLASTIC BLADE. Process remaining tablespoon of butter until smooth. Add the flour and blend. Add the butter-flour mixture to the peas and cook 5 minutes longer.

4 servings.

Zucchini au Gratin

4 small zucchini, peeled
1 tablespoon butter
1 teaspoon salt
½ teaspoon Tellicherry pepper
3 eggs
1 tablespoon flour
1 cup milk
6 ounces Gruyère cheese

Preheat oven to 400°.

Insert SLICING DISK. Using heavy pressure, slice the zucchini.

Melt the butter in a saucepan. Add the zucchini and sprinkle with salt and pepper. Cover and cook over low heat, stirring from time to time, until zucchini is soft and mushy. Drain.

Insert STEEL BLADE. Beat the eggs. Insert FUNNEL. Add the flour, milk and zucchini, and puree. Pour into a buttered baking dish.

Insert SHREDDING DISK. Shred the cheese. Sprinkle over the zucchini. Bake for 20 minutes, or until cheese is melted and casserole is slightly puffed.

4 servings.

Pureed Asparagus

2 ounces Parmesan cheese
2 pounds cooked asparagus
1 tablespoon flour
2 tablespoons butter
¼ teaspoon nutmeg
1 teaspoon salt
½ teaspoon Tellicherry pepper
1 cup heavy cream

Preheat broiler.

Insert STEEL BLADE. Using the on/off method, grate the cheese. Set aside.

Keep the STEEL BLADE in place. Using the on/off method, chop the asparagus, then puree. Add the remaining ingredients except the cheese.

Turn into an au gratin pan or into individual au gratins. Sprinkle with the cheese. Place under the broiler until cheese melts and turns golden brown.

6 servings.

Cauliflower Allemand

1 medium head cauliflower
1 small shallot
2 tablespoons melted butter
2 tablespoons flour
1 cup chicken broth
1 teaspoon lemon juice
1 egg yolk
3 ounces Parmesan cheese

To boil cauliflower: Remove leaves, cut off stalk and soak in cold water for 30 minutes, head down. Cook, head up, in boiling salted water for 20 minutes. Drain.

To steam cauliflower: Cover the bottom of the steamer with hot water and bring to a boil. Place the cauliflower on the rack and steam for 20 minutes. Drain.

Preheat oven to 350°.

Separate the cooked cauliflower into florets and place in a greased baking dish.

Insert STEEL BLADE. Using the on/off method, finely chop the shallot, then add the butter. Insert FUNNEL. With the motor on, add the flour, chicken broth, lemon juice and egg yolk. Process until smooth. Pour over the cauliflower.

Insert STEEL BLADE. Using the on/off method, grate the cheese. Sprinkle over the cauliflower. Bake about 15 minutes until cheese is melted.

6 servings.

Red Cabbage and Apples

6 slices bacon
1 large onion
1 small head red cabbage
2 tart green apples, peeled and cored
¼ cup water
1 tablespoon sugar
1 teaspoon salt
½ teaspoon Tellicherry pepper
¼ teaspoon nutmeg

Fry the bacon until crisp. Reserve the drippings.

Insert STEEL BLADE. Using the on/off method, chop the onion. Add the bacon and drippings, then give the blade another turn or two. Place in a heavy pan. Cook over low heat, stirring frequently, until onion becomes soft.

Insert THIN SLICING DISK. Using light pressure, slice the cabbage. Add to the onion. Lower the heat, cover and cook without stirring for 15 minutes. Shake the casserole occasionally and, if necessary, add a little more water.

Keep THIN SLICING DISK in place. Using light pressure, slice the apples. Add to the cabbage along with the water, sugar, salt, pepper and nutmeg. Stir to blend. Cover and simmer over low heat for 1½ hours.

4 servings.

Pea Timbales

2 tablespoons butter
1 2/3 cups cooked peas
2 eggs
1 teaspoon dried basil
1 teaspoon salt
¼ teaspoon Muntok (or white) pepper

Sauce:
3 tablespoons flour
¼ teaspoon Muntok (or white) pepper
1 cup milk
3 tablespoons melted butter
1/3 cup cooked peas

Preheat oven to 350°.

Insert STEEL BLADE. Using the on/off method, cream the butter. Add 1 2/3 cups peas and puree. With the motor on, add the eggs, basil, salt and pepper.

Pour into individual buttered molds. Cover each mold with buttered paper. Set the molds in a pan of hot water and bake until firm, about 30 minutes.

To make sauce, insert STEEL BLADE. Add the flour and pepper. With the motor on, add the milk and melted butter. Process until smooth.

Pour into a saucepan and bring to a boil, stirring constantly. Boil for 2 minutes. Add the 1/3 cup peas and pour sauce over the unmolded timbales.

4 servings.

String Beans and Cream Sauce

1 pound green beans, trimmed
2 tablespoons butter
2 tablespoons flour
1 cup chicken broth
2 teaspoons lemon juice
1 teaspoon salt
½ teaspoon Tellicherry pepper
1 egg yolk
½ cup heavy cream
1 tablespoon dried basil

Insert SLICING DISK. Using heavy pressure, slice the beans horizontally (French slice). Place in a saucepan with boiling water to cover. Bring to a boil for 2 minutes, then drain. Place in an ovenproof serving dish.

Insert STEEL BLADE. Process butter until smooth, then add the flour. With the motor on, add the chicken broth, lemon juice, salt and pepper. Pour into a saucepan and bring to a boil.

Keep STEEL BLADE in place. Beat the egg yolk, then add ¼ cup of the hot broth mixture. Pour this mixture into the broth mixture in the saucepan. Stir in the heavy cream and pour over the beans. Heat thoroughly.

Keep STEEL BLADE in place. Using the on/off method, mince the basil. Sprinkle over the beans before serving.

4 servings.

Variation

Sliced mushrooms can also be added to the broth and brought to a boil.

Salads

Tuna Fish Salad

1 can (7 ounces) tuna fish
2 scallions
3 stalks celery
½ medium green pepper
1 hard-boiled egg
½ cup mayonnaise
Salt and pepper to taste

If tuna is packed in oil, put it in a strainer and pour boiling water over it to remove oil. Drain.

Insert SLICING DISK. Using light pressure, slice the scallions, celery and green pepper.

Insert PLASTIC BLADE. Add the egg, mayonnaise, salt and pepper, and process until well mixed. Add the tuna and give the blade another turn or two.

This can be served as an entree, used to stuff tomatoes or zucchini or as a sandwich filler.

2-3 servings.

Lobster or Crab Salad

1 cup cooked lobster or crabmeat
4 stalks celery
2 scallions
¼ cup mayonnaise
Salt and Muntok (or white) pepper to taste

Insert SLICING DISK. Using heavy pressure, slice the lobster or crabmeat, celery and scallions.

Insert PLASTIC BLADE. Add the mayonnaise to the mixture and process until well mixed. Add the salt and pepper, and give the blade another turn or two.

This can be served as an entree, or as a stuffing for tomatoes, avocado or zucchini. Also very good on toasted rolls for sandwiches.

2-3 servings.

Beet and Cucumber Salad

4 cooked beets
1 small cucumber (peel if waxed)
1 small onion
1 tablespoon dried coriander
1 teaspoon salt
4 sprigs parsley or dill
1 cup yogurt
1 bunch watercress

Insert SLICING DISK. Using light pressure, slice the beets, cucumber and onion. Remove and sprinkle with coriander and salt.

Insert STEEL BLADE. Using the on/off method, mince the parsley or dill. Add the yogurt and mix well.

Make a bed of watercress and arrange the beet, cucumber and onion slices alternately. Top with the yogurt mixture.

4 servings.

Shrimp and Avocado Salad

2 ripe avocados
Juice of ½ lemon
4 sprigs parsley
1 cup cottage cheese
¼ cup mayonnaise
1 teaspoon dried basil
1 pound cooked shrimp
Romaine, Boston or bibb lettuce

Peel the avocados, cut in half and remove the pits.

Insert SLICING DISK. Using firm pressure, slice the avocados. Remove and sprinkle with all but 2 tablespoons of the lemon juice.

Insert STEEL BLADE. Using the on/off method, chop the parsley. Add the cottage cheese and the remaining lemon juice, and process until mixture is the consistency of sour cream. Add the mayonnaise and basil. Mix well.

Make a bed of lettuce on a serving plate. Place the shrimp and the avocado slices alternately around the edge of the dish. Mound the dressing in the center.

4 servings.

Chicken Salad

1 pound cooked chicken
½ bunch celery
5 hard-boiled eggs
½ cup butter
1 cup vinegar
2 tablespoons horseradish
1 teaspoon Dijon mustard
1 tablespoon salt
1 teaspoon Tellicherry pepper

Insert SLICING DISK. Using heavy pressure, slice the chicken and celery. Set aside.

Insert STEEL BLADE. Add remaining ingredients and, using the on/off method, process until eggs are finely chopped. Add the chicken and celery, and give the blade another turn or two. This can be served as an entree, stuffing for tomatoes or in sandwiches.

Variation

Use mayonnaise and minced onion in place of the vinegar, horseradish and mustard.

4 servings.

Radish and Cucumber Salad

2 medium cucumbers
2 bunches radishes
1 teaspoon salt
1 cup yogurt
2 tablespoons tarragon vinegar
1 teaspoon celery seeds
½ teaspoon Tellicherry pepper

Peel the cucumbers if waxed. Slice in half lengthwise. Using a teaspoon, remove seeds.

Insert THIN SLICING DISK. Using medium pressure, slice the cucumbers. Insert FUNNEL. Using medium pressure, slice the radishes. Remove and sprinkle with salt. Chill for 30 minutes and drain.

Insert PLASTIC BLADE. Add the yogurt and, with the motor on, add the vinegar, celery seeds and pepper, and mix well. Add the cucumbers and radishes and, using the on/off method, mix well.

6 servings.

Cole Slaw

1 slice onion
½ small head cabbage
2 medium carrots
½ small green pepper
¼ cup mayonnaise

Insert STEEL BLADE. Using the on/off method, chop the onion.

Insert SLICING DISK. Using light pressure, slice the cabbage.

Insert SHREDDING DISK. Shred the carrots and green pepper.

Insert PLASTIC BLADE. Using the on/off method, blend all ingredients until vegetables are thoroughly coated with mayonnaise.

4 servings.

Spinach Salad

1 pound fresh spinach
½ pound large mushrooms
6 strips crisp cooked bacon
2 hard-boiled eggs

Dressing:
1 egg yolk
¾ cup vegetable oil
¼ cup wine vinegar
2 tablespoon sugar
½ teaspoon salt
¼ teaspoon Tellicherry pepper

Wash and dry the spinach (a salad spinner comes in handy here). Break into bite-size pieces.

Insert SLICING DISK. Using heavy pressure, slice the mushrooms. Set aside.

Insert STEEL BLADE. Using the on/off method, finely chop together the bacon and eggs. Set aside.

To make the dressing, insert PLASTIC BLADE. Beat the egg yolk. Add the oil, vinegar, sugar, salt and pepper. Mix well.

Toss together all the ingredients in a salad bowl.

6 servings.

Ham Salad

4 ounces Cheddar cheese
6 hard-boiled eggs
4 scallions
4 stalks celery
1 pound cooked ham
½ cup pineapple chunks
½ cup mayonnaise
1 tablespoon lemon juice
1 teaspoon Dijon mustard

Insert SHREDDING DISK. Shred the cheese. Set aside.

Insert STEEL BLADE. Using the on/off method, chop the eggs, scallions and celery until chunky. Add the ham and continue to use the on/off method until ham is coarsley chopped. Set aside.

Insert PLASTIC BLADE. Using the on/off method, process the remaining ingredients until the pineapple is the same consistency as the ham. Add the ham mixture and cheese, and continue to use the on/off method until well mixed.

5-6 servings.

Avocado, Mushroom and Tomato Salad

1 ripe avocado
6 large mushrooms
2 ripe tomatoes
1 large shallot
4 sprigs dill
¼ cup olive oil
2 tablespoons lemon juice
1 teaspoon salt
½ teaspoon Tellicherry pepper

Peel the avocado, cut in half and remove the pit.

Insert THIN SLICING DISK. Using heavy pressure, slice the avocado and mushrooms.

Insert FRENCH FRY SLICER. Slice the tomatoes. Set vegetables aside.

Insert STEEL BLADE. Using the on/off method, mince together the shallot and dill. Add the oil, lemon juice, salt and pepper, and mix well. Pour over the combined vegetables. Serve chilled.

4–6 servings.

Salad Dressings, Sauces and Gravies

Raisin Sauce

1 slice ginger root (the size of a half dollar)
1 cup sugar
1 cup raisins
2 tablespoons vinegar
½ teaspoon salt
½ teaspoon cinnamon
¼ teaspoon cloves
½ cup water
1 cup currant jelly

Insert STEEL BLADE. Using the on/off method, mince the ginger root. Add the sugar and raisins, and give the blade another turn or two. Add the vinegar, salt, cinnamon and cloves, and process until well mixed.

Add to the water in a saucepan and bring mixture to a boil. Stir in jelly. When the jelly has melted, sauce is ready to serve over baked ham.

Yields 2 cups.

Italian Dressing

1 clove garlic
1 cup vegetable oil
¼ cup vinegar
1 teaspoon salt
½ teaspoon pepper
½ teaspoon celery salt
¼ teaspoon cayenne
¼ teaspoon dry mustard
Dash of hot pepper sauce

Insert STEEL BLADE. Using the on/off method, mince the garlic.

Insert PLASTIC BLADE and FUNNEL. While the motor is on, add the remaining ingredients and blend well. Chill. Shake before serving.

Yields 1 cup.

French Dressing

½ cup vegetable oil
2 tablespoons vinegar
2 tablespoons lemon juice
2 teaspoons sugar
½ teaspoon salt
½ teaspoon dry mustard
½ teaspoon paprika
Dash of cayenne

Insert PLASTIC BLADE. Process all the ingredients until well mixed. Chill.

Yields ¾ cup.

Creamy French Dressing

Omit the dry mustard and add 1 tablespoon mayonnaise and ½ teaspoon catsup.

Blue Cheese Dressing

1 clove garlic
6 ounces blue cheese
½ cup mayonnaise
½ cup sour cream
Juice of ½ lemon
¼ teaspoon pepper
1/8 teaspoon salt
1/3 cup milk

Insert STEEL BLADE. Using the on/off method, mince together the garlic and 4 ounces of the cheese.

Insert PLASTIC BLADE. Add the mayonnaise and sour cream, and process until well mixed. Add the lemon juice, pepper and salt and, with the motor on, add the milk and remaining 2 ounces of the blue cheese. Two or three turns of the blade and the dressing is ready.

If you prefer the dressing smooth, not chunky, add all the blue cheese with the garlic.

Chill. It may be necessary to stir dressing before serving because it gets very thick after it has been refrigerated.

Yields 1½ cups.

Cherry Sauce

1 can (1 pound) waterpacked pitted sour cherries*
1 slice ginger root (the size of a quarter)
½ cup pine nuts
1 orange, rind and juice
¼ cup sugar
2 tablespoons cornstarch
½ teaspoon salt
¼ cup currant jelly
2 tablespoons dry sherry

Drain the cherries. Reserve the liquid.

Insert STEEL BLADE. Using the on/off method, mince the ginger root. Add the pine nuts and continue to use the on/off method until finely chopped. Set aside.

Keep the STEEL BLADE in place. Using the on/off method, grate the orange rind with the sugar. Add the pine nuts and ginger root and, with the motor on, add the cornstarch, salt, orange juice and reserved cherry liquid.

Pour into a saucepan and cook over medium heat, stirring constantly, until mixture thickens. Add the cherries and currant jelly. Just before serving, add the sherry. Serve with roast duckling or any roasted game hen.

4 servings.

*If unable to obtain waterpacked, omit the sugar from the recipe.

Mayonnaise

1 egg
1 tablespoon lemon juice or vinegar
½ teaspoon salt
¼ teaspoon dry mustard
1 cup vegetable oil

Insert PLASTIC BLADE. Mix together the egg, lemon juice or vinegar, salt and mustard. Insert FUNNEL and, with the motor on, pour in the oil slowly in a steady stream. The longer the mayonnaise is processed the thicker it becomes. Refrigerate.

This mayonnaise will last about 2 weeks and will not separate under refrigeration.

Herb Mayonnaise

After the mayonnaise has been made, add 3 or 4 tablespoons of herbs such as tarragon, basil, chervil, chives or parsley.

Yields 1 cup.

Note: If fresh herbs are used, they should be blanched.

White Sauce

1 tablespoon flour
¼ teaspoon salt
1/8 teaspoon Muntok (or white) pepper
2 tablespoons melted butter
1 cup milk

Insert PLASTIC BLADE. Mix together the flour, salt and pepper. With the motor on, add the melted butter to form a paste. Add the milk and process until smooth.

Pour into a saucepan and bring to a boil, stirring constantly. Boil 2 minutes.

Yields 1 cup.

White Sauce for Vegetables and Fish

Increase the flour to 2 tablespoons.

Cream Sauce

Substitute cream for the milk.

Thousand Island Dressing

¼ small onion
½ stalk celery
¼ medium-size green pepper
2 hard-boiled eggs
1 cup mayonnaise
¼ cup chili sauce
1 teaspoon paprika
½ teaspoon salt

Insert STEEL BLADE. Using the on/off method, mince together the onion, celery and green pepper.

Insert PLASTIC BLADE. Add the remaining ingredients and process until well mixed. Chill.

Yields 2 cups.

Brown Sauce or Gravy

3 tablespoons flour
¼ teaspoon salt
1/8 teaspoon Tellicherry pepper
4 tablespoons butter
1 cup brown stock or water

Brown the flour in a heavy skillet over low heat.

Insert PLASTIC BLADE. Mix together the flour, salt and pepper. With the motor on, add the butter and stock or water.

Pour into the skillet and bring to a boil. Boil for 2 minutes, stirring constantly.

Yields 1 cup.

Grand Marnier Sauce

4 egg yolks
¾ cup sugar
1 tablespoon lemon juice
¼ teaspoon salt
2 tablespoons flour
¾ cup Grand Marnier
2 cups heavy cream

Insert STEEL BLADE. Beat the egg yolks. Mix in the sugar, lemon juice, salt and flour. Remove to a bain-marie or double boiler. Cook over hot water, stirring constantly. Add the Grand Marnier and cook until sauce thickens. Cool.

Keep STEEL BLADE in place. Whip the cream. Fold into the Grand Marnier mixture. Chill. Spoon over fresh fruit.

Yields 2 cups.

Tartar Sauce

1 small pickle
1 pearl onion
1 stalk celery
1 tablespoon capers
2 sprigs parsley
1 cup mayonnaise

Insert STEEL BLADE. Using the on/off method, finely chop together the pickle, onion, celery, capers and parsley.

Insert PLASTIC BLADE. Add the mayonnaise and mix well. Serve with fish.

Yields 1 cup.

Chocolate Fudge Sauce

1 ounce semi-sweet chocolate
1 cup sugar
1 tablespoon butter
1/3 cup boiling water
2 tablespoons corn syrup
½ teaspoon vanilla
1/8 teaspoon salt

Insert STEEL BLADE. Using the on/off method, grate the chocolate with the sugar. Add the butter and, with the motor on, add the boiling water and corn syrup. Blend well.

Pour into a saucepan and bring to a boil. Boil for 5 minutes. Remove from heat and add the vanilla and salt.

To reheat, place in the top of a double boiler over hot water.

Yields 1 cup.

Crimson Sauce

½ cup raspberry jam
Juice of 1 small lemon
Pinch of salt
1/3 cup water
1 tablespoon butter

Insert PLASTIC BLADE. Blend together the first 4 ingredients. Pour into a saucepan and heat through over medium heat. Stir in the butter until melted.

6 servings (about ½ cup).

Mushroom Sauce

½ pound mushrooms
3 tablespoons butter
3 tablespoons flour
1 cup light cream
1 teaspoon salt
½ teaspoon Tellicherry pepper

Insert SLICING DISK. Using heavy pressure, slice the mushrooms.

Melt the butter in a skillet and sauté the mushrooms over high heat until golden brown. Reduce heat to low.

Insert PLASTIC BLADE. Add the flour and, with the motor on, blend in the cream, salt and pepper. Add to the mushrooms and continue to cook sauce until thick. Serve with beef or chicken.

Yields 1½ cups.

Variation

Add 1 tablespoon of Madeira, brandy or cognac just before serving.

Breads

Blueberry Muffins

2 cups flour
4 teaspoons baking powder
½ teaspoon salt
2 tablespoons sugar
2 tablespoons butter
1 egg
1 cup milk
1 cup blueberries

Preheat oven to 350°.

Sift together the flour, baking powder and salt.

Insert STEEL BLADE. Cream together the sugar and butter. Insert FUNNEL and add the egg. With the motor on, add the sifted dry ingredients alternately with the milk. Process until just blended. Add the blueberries and give the blade another turn or two.

Fill greased muffin tins 2/3 full. Bake until browned, about 20 to 25 minutes.

Yields 1 dozen.

Bran Muffins

1 cup flour
2 cups bran
1½ teaspoons baking soda
1 teaspoon baking powder
½ teaspoon salt
1 egg
½ cup molasses
1 cup milk
½ cup raisins (optional)

Preheat oven to 375°.

Sift together the flour, bran, baking soda, baking powder and salt.

Insert STEEL BLADE. Beat the egg. Insert FUNNEL and add the molasses. Add the bran alternately with the milk. Add the sifted dry ingredients. Add the raisins. Give blade another turn or two.

Fill greased muffin tins 2/3 full. Bake until lightly browned, about 30 minutes.

Yields 2 dozen.

Baking Powder Biscuits

2 cups flour
4 teaspoons baking powder
1 teaspoon salt
2 tablespoons shortening
2/3 cup milk

Preheat oven to 450°.

Sift togther the flour, baking powder and salt.

Insert STEEL BLADE. Cream the shortening until smooth. Insert FUNNEL and with the motor on, add the dry ingredients alternately with the milk. Process until a ball forms.

Turn out onto a floured board and roll out ¾ inch thick. Cut with a biscuit cutter and place on an ungreased cookie sheet. Bake until golden brown, about 12 to 15 minutes.

Yields 1 dozen.

Swedish Rye Bread

1 package dry yeast
¼ cup warm water
2 tablespoons shortening
1 cup rye flour
¼ cup molasses
1 teaspoon salt
¾ cup boiling water
2 cups unbleached flour
1 egg, lightly beaten

Dissolve yeast in the warm water.

Insert STEEL BLADE. Using the on/off method, cut the shortening into the rye flour. Insert FUNNEL and, with the motor on, add the molasses, salt and boiling water. Process until well blended. Set aside to cool.

Sift the unbleached flour.

Keep STEEL BLADE in place. Add the sifted flour and, with the motor on, add the yeast mixture. Add the cooled rye mixture and, using the on/off method, knead the dough until it forms a ball.

Remove. Cover and let rest for 10 minutes. Knead on a floured board until smooth. Put the dough in a greased bowl. Cover and let rise in a warm place until doubled. Punch down the dough, cover and let rise again until doubled.

Punch down the dough. Shape into a loaf and place in a greased pan (9 by 5 by 3 inches). Let rise until doubled, about 30 minutes.

Preheat oven to 350°.

Brush loaf with lightly beaten egg. Bake for 40 minutes, until the bread pulls away from the sides of the pan and sounds hollow when rapped.

Yields 1 loaf.

Apple Nut Bread

2 large tart apples
2½ cups flour
1 teaspoon salt
1 teaspoon baking powder
1 teaspoon baking soda
¾ cup walnuts or pecans
1 cup sugar
3 tablespoons butter
3 eggs
1 cup buttermilk
1 teaspoon vanilla

Preheat oven to 350°.

Peel the apples if waxed. Core.

Sift together the flour, salt, baking powder and soda.

Insert STEEL BLADE. Using the on/off method, coarsely chop together the apples and nuts. Set aside.

Keep STEEL BLADE in place. Cream together the sugar and butter. Insert FUNNEL. Add the eggs and process until mixture is lemon colored. With the motor on, add the sifted dry ingredients alternately with the buttermilk. Add the apples, nuts and vanilla, and give the blade another turn or two.

Pour into a greased 10-inch loaf pan and bake for 1 hour, until bread pulls away from the sides of the pan or a knife inserted in the center comes out clean. Cool in the pan for 5 minutes. Loosen from the sides, turn out on a rack and cool completely before slicing.

The bread takes on more flavor if allowed to mature for 24 hours.

Yields 1 loaf.

Herb Bread

1 package dry yeast
2 teaspoons sugar
1 cup warm water
3 cups flour
1½ teaspoons salt
1 tablespoon shortening
1 teaspoon dried drill
1 teaspoon dried thyme
½ teaspoon dried rosemary
½ teaspoon dried tarragon
2 tablespoons sesame or poppy seeds

Dissolve the yeast and sugar in the warm water.

Sift together the flour and salt.

Insert STEEL BLADE. Cream the shortening. Using the on/off method, add the dill, thyme, rosemary and tarragon. Add 1 cup of the sifted dry ingredients and process until mixed. Add the remaining dry ingredients alternately with the yeast mixture. Using the on/off method, process until the dough is soft.

Turn out onto a floured board and knead until smooth and elastic. Put the dough in a greased bowl. Cover and let rise in a warm place until doubled.

Punch down the dough. Shape into an 18-inch roll. Place on a greased baking sheet. With a sharp knife, make ¼-inch-deep slashes in the top of the loaf 1½ inches apart. Brush the top with water. Let rise again until double.

Preheat the oven to 425°.

Brush the top of the loaf with water again. Bake for 15 minutes. Brush the top with water again, and sprinkle with seeds. Bake until bread sounds hollow when tapped, about another 15 minutes.

Yields 1 large loaf.

Bread Sticks

1 package dry yeast
3 tablespoons warm water
½ cup milk
2 tablespoons butter
1 tablespoon sugar
½ teaspoon salt
3 egg whites
3 cups sifted flour
1 tablespoon sea salt

Dissolve the yeast in the warm water.

Scald the milk. Cool to lukewarm. Add the butter, sugar, salt and yeast mixture.

Insert STEEL BLADE. Beat 2 of the egg whites with a pinch of salt until shiny. Insert FUNNEL and with the motor on, add the sifted flour alternately with the liquid. Using the on/off method, knead the dough until a ball forms.

Turn into a greased bowl, cover and let rise in a warm place until doubled.

Punch down the dough. Roll into sticks about 8 inches long, rounding the ends. Place on a lightly greased cookie sheet about 1 inch apart. Let rise for 30 minutes.

Preheat oven to 425°.

Bake for 5 minutes. Reduce heat to 350°. Brush the bread sticks with the remaining egg white and sprinkle with sea salt. Bake 4 minutes longer until crisp.

Yields 2 dozen.

Variations

Sprinkle with Parmesan cheese or salt and cayenne.

White Bread

1 package dry yeast
3 teaspoons sugar
½ cup warm water
1 cup milk
3½ cups flour
1 teaspoon salt
1 tablespoon lard

Dissolve the yeast and sugar in the warm water.

Scald the milk. Cool.

Sift together the flour and salt.

Insert STEEL BLADE. Using the on/off method, cut the lard into ½ cup of the sifted dry ingredients. Add the remaining dry ingredients alternately with the cooled milk. Add the yeast mixture and process until a ball forms.

Turn out onto a floured board. Cover and let rest 10 minutes. Place in a greased bowl and let rise in a warm place until doubled. Punch down the dough, cover and let rise again for 30 minutes.

Punch down the dough. Shape into a loaf. Let rise 15 to 20 minutes.

Preheat oven to 425°.

Bake for 30 minutes, until bread sounds hollow when rapped.

Yields 1 loaf.

Cranberry Bread

2 cups flour
1½ teaspoons baking powder
½ teaspoon baking soda
½ teaspoon salt
2 oranges, rind and juice
¾ cup walnuts
2 cups fresh cranberries
1 cup sugar
4 tablespoons butter
1 egg

Preheat oven to 350°.

Sift together the flour, baking powder, soda and salt.

Insert SHREDDING DISK. Shred the nuts. Set aside.

Insert SLICING DISK. Using light pressure, slice the cranberries. Set aside.

Insert STEEL BLADE. Process the orange rind and sugar until rind is in very small pieces. Using the on/off method, blend in the butter until smooth. Add the egg. Add the sifted dry ingredients alternately with the orange juice. Add the nuts and cranberries, and process until just blended.

Pour into a greased loaf pan (9 by 5 by 3 inches) and bake for 1 hour, until knife inserted in the center comes out clean.

Yields 1 loaf.

Ripe Olive Bread

3 cups flour
1 teaspoon salt
1 teaspoon baking powder
2 cups pitted black olives
3 eggs
2 tablespoons sugar
3 tablespoons olive oil
¾ cup milk

Preheat oven to 350°.

Sift together the flour, salt and baking powder.

Insert SLICING DISK. Using heavy pressure, slice the olives. Set aside.

Insert STEEL BLADE. Beat the eggs. Insert FUNNEL and, with the motor on, add the sugar and oil. Add the sifted dry ingredients alternately with the milk and olives.

Pour into a greased loaf pan (9 by 5 by 3 inches). Let stand 20 minutes. Bake until bread sounds hollow when rapped, about 1 hour.

Excellent thinly sliced and served with cheese.

Yields 1 loaf.

Orange Muffins

2 oranges
1¾ cups flour
1½ teaspoons baking powder
¼ teaspoon salt
¾ cup sugar
1/3 cup butter
2 egg yolks
¼ cup milk
1 teaspoon vanilla

Preheat oven to 350°.

Zest 1 orange and juice both oranges.

Sift together the flour, baking powder and salt.

Insert STEEL BLADE. Using the on/off method, finely grate the orange rind with the sugar. Cream the butter with the sugar mixture. Add the egg yolks and milk. Insert FUNNEL and, with the motor on, add the sifted dry ingredients alternately with the orange juice. Add the vanilla and give the blade another turn or two.

Fill greased muffin tins 2/3 full. Bake until golden brown, about 30 minutes.

Yields 1 dozen.

Desserts

Almond Paste Cookies

2 cups hazelnuts
2½ cups sugar
2 cups blanched almonds
1 teaspoon almond extract
4 egg whites

Preheat oven to 400°.

Insert STEEL BLADE. Using the on/off method, finely chop the hazelnuts. Set aside on a flat plate.

Keep STEEL BLADE in place. Process the sugar until superfine. Add the almonds and, using the on/off method, finely chop. Add the extract and process until mixture is powdered. Set aside.

Keep STEEL BLADE in place. Beat egg whites with a pinch of salt until soft peaks form. Slowly add the almond powder and process until well blended.

Drop by teaspoonfuls into the hazelnuts and gently roll to coat. Place on lightly greased cookie sheets 1 inch apart. Flatten slightly with the back of a spoon. Bake for 10 minutes, until golden brown.

Yields 3 dozen.

Lemon Sponge Cake

1¾ cups sifted flour
2 teaspoons baking powder
½ teaspoon salt
1 large lemon, rind and juice
6 eggs, separated
1½ cups sugar

Frosting and filling:
1 quart strawberries
2 cups heavy cream
½ cup confectioners' sugar
½ teaspoon vanilla

Glaze:
¼ cup currant jelly
1 tablespoon lemon juice

Preheat oven to 350°.

Sift together the flour, baking powder and salt.

Insert STEEL BLADE. Beat the egg whites with a pinch of salt until the whites start to roll. While the motor is on, add ¾ cup of the sugar slowly. Beat until whites form stiff peaks. Set aside.

Keep STEEL BLADE in place. Beat the egg yolks until thick and lemon colored, slowly add the remaining sugar while continuing to beat. Insert FUNNEL. Add the sifted dry ingredients alternately with the lemon juice, reserving 1 tablespoon for the glaze. When all the flour has been incorporated, fold into the egg whites.

Pour into an ungreased 10-inch tube pan. Bake for 40 minutes, until cake springs back at the touch of a finger. Remove from oven. Invert the pan and cool cake thoroughly. Slice into 3 layers.

To make frosting, insert SLICING DISK. Using medium pressure, slice ¾ of the strawberries. Set aside.

Insert STEEL BLADE. Whip the cream until it is the consistency of sour cream. Add the confectioners' sugar slowly. Add the vanilla and give the blade another turn or two.

Place a layer of sliced strawberries and a layer of whipped cream between each layer of the cake. Use the balance of the whipped cream to frost and decorate with any remaining strawberries.

To make glaze, melt the jelly with the reserved tablespoon of lemon juice. Coat the reserved berries and use to decorate the cake.

12 servings.

Pie Crust

½ cup butter or shortening
1½ cups sifted flour
¼ cup cold water

Cut the butter or shortening into cubes.

Insert STEEL BLADE. Feed the butter or shortening around the bowl and add the flour. Using the on/off method, cut the butter into the flour until mixture is consistency of coarse meal. While the motor is on, pour in the water. Process until a ball forms above the blade. The dough will be moist. Do not overprocess or the crust will be tough.

The dough does not need to be refrigerated before rolling out on a floured board. Prick the crust several times before baking.

Yields pastry for 9-inch 1-crust pie.

Gingerbread

2½ cups flour
1 teaspoon baking soda
½ teaspoon salt
1 teaspoon ginger
¼ teaspoon ground cloves
4 tablespoons butter
1 cup molasses
½ cup boiling water

Preheat oven to 350°.

Sift together the flour, baking soda, salt and spices.

Insert STEEL BLADE. Cream the butter. Insert FUNNEL. With the motor on, add the sifted dry ingredients alternately with the molasses and water. Process until well mixed.

Pour into a buttered 9-inch-square cake pan. Bake 30 minutes, until a cake tester comes out clean.

Yields one 9-inch-square gingerbread.

Frozen Strawberry Dessert

1 quart strawberries
1 tablespoon sugar
3 egg whites
½ cup heavy cream
1 cup sugar
1 tablespoon lemon juice
1 teaspoon vanilla

Reserve 12 whole berries for decorating.

Insert SLICING DISK. Using heavy pressure, slice the remaining berries. Remove to a bowl and sprinkle with 1 tablespoon sugar.

Insert STEEL BLADE. Beat the egg whites with a pinch of salt until stiff. Set aside.

Keep STEEL BLADE in place. Whip the cream. When it is the consistency of sour cream, slowly add the sugar while the motor is on. Add the lemon juice, sliced strawberries and egg whites. Add the vanilla and give the blade another turn or two.

Fill parfait or champagne glasses that have been chilled. Decorate with reserved whole berries.

12 servings.

Frozen Strawberry Pie

Make a crust with the following:
½ cup fine chopped walnuts
2 tablespoons butter
3½ ounces coconut

Preheat oven to 325°.

Insert STEEL BLADE. Chop the walnuts. Mix in the butter. Add the coconut and give the blade another turn or two.

Press mixture firmly into a 9-inch pie plate. Bake for 10 to 15 minutes, or until golden brown. Cool.

Fill with Frozen Strawberry Dessert filling (above). Decorate with reserved whole berries. Place in the freezer until a few minutes before serving.

Chocolate Cake

1½ cups flour
3 teaspoons baking powder
2 ounces unsweetened chocolate
1 cup sugar
2 cups butter
2 eggs
½ cup milk
1 teaspoon vanilla

Preheat oven to 350°.

Sift together the flour, baking powder and salt.

Insert STEEL BLADE. Using the on/off method, grate the chocolate with the sugar. Add the butter and continue to use the on/off method until mixture is creamy. Insert FUNNEL. With the motor on, add the eggs. Add the sifted dry ingredients alternately with the milk. Add the vanilla.

Pour into 2 greased 8-inch layer cake pans. Bake for 20 minutes, until a cake tester comes out clean. Cool before frosting.

Yields one 8-inch 2-layer cake.

Chocolate Frosting

2 cups confectioners' sugar
4 tablespoons butter
½ cup cocoa
½ cup evaporated milk
1 tablespoon chocolate liqueur

Insert STEEL BLADE. Using the on/off method, cream together the sugar and butter. Add the cocoa and milk. Process until mixture is light and fluffy. Add the chocolate liqueur and give the blade another turn or two.

Additional milk or cocoa can be added to achieve desired consistency or taste.

Yields frosting for 8-inch 2-layer cake.

110

Walnut Spice Cake

1½ cups walnuts
1½ teaspoons baking soda
1½ cups warm water
1½ cups raisins
2 cups flour
¼ teaspoon salt
1½ teaspoons cinnamon
1½ teaspoons ginger
1½ teaspoons nutmeg
1½ cups brown sugar
¾ cup butter
3 eggs
1½ teaspoons lemon juice
1½ teaspoons vanilla extract

Cream Cheese Frosting:
8 ounces cream cheese
2/3 cup butter
3 cups confectioners' sugar
3 teaspoons vanilla extract

Insert SHREDDING DISK. Shred the nuts.

Add the baking soda to the warm water. Add the raisins.

Sift together the flour, salt and spices.

Insert STEEL BLADE. Using the on/off method, cream together the sugar and butter. Insert FUNNEL. Add the eggs, lemon juice and vanilla. With the motor on, add the sifted dry ingredients alternately with the water-raisin mixture. Add the nuts and give the blade another turn or two.

Grease and lightly flour three 8-inch cake pans. Pour in the batter. Bake 25 to 30 minutes, until cake tester comes out clean. Cool.

To make frosting, insert STEEL BLADE. Using the on/off method, beat together the cream cheese and butter until fluffy. Insert FUNNEL and, with the motor on, slowly add the confectioners' sugar. Add the vanilla and give the blade another turn or two.

Frost between each layer, then frost sides and top of the cake.

To decorate, chop walnuts and sprinkle all over, or melt 2 squares of semi-sweet chocolate and swirl over the top.

Yields one 8-inch 3-layer cake.

Apple Pie

Pastry for 9-inch 2-crust pie (see page 108)
1 lemon, rind and juice
6 to 8 medium-sized tart apples
½ cup sugar
½ teaspoon cinnamon
¼ teaspoon salt
½ tablespoon butter

Preheat oven to 450°.

Line a pie plate with half the pastry.

Peel the apples if waxed. Cut them in half and core.

Insert SLICING DISK. Using heavy pressure, slice the apples. Remove to pastry-lined pie plate.

Insert STEEL BLADE. Using the on/off method, grate the lemon rind with the sugar. Add the lemon juice, cinnamon and salt. Pour over the apples.

Cover with the top crust. Dot with butter. Bake 10 minutes. Reduce heat to 350° and bake until golden, about 30 minutes longer.

Yields one 9-inch pie.

Variations

Add a small amount of sugar and cinnamon to the pastry for extra flavor.

Add 2 tablespoons grated Cheddar cheese to the dry ingredients in the pastry.

Plum Flan

1¼ cups flour
½ teaspoon baking powder
½ teaspoon salt
½ teaspoon cinnamon
1 cup sugar
½ cup butter
1 pound fresh plums
1 egg
1 cup heavy cream

Preheat oven to 375°.

Sift together the flour, baking powder, salt and cinnamon.

Insert STEEL BLADE. Using the on/off method, cream together the sugar and butter. Add the sifted dry ingredients. Process until well mixed.

Reserve 1/3 of the crust mixture. Cover the bottom of baking dish (8 by 8 by 2 inches) with the remaining crust mixture and press until it comes 1 inch up the sides.

Cut the plums in half and remove the pits. Arrange in a single layer over the crust, skin side up. Sprinkle with the remaining crust mixture. Bake for 15 minutes.

While the flan is baking, insert PLASTIC BLADE. Beat the egg. Blend in the cream. Pour over the plums after they have baked for 15 minutes. Return to the oven and bake 25 minutes longer. Cool and cut into squares.

12 servings.

Molasses Cookies

½ cup butter or shortening
3 teaspoons baking soda
¼ cup cold water
2 cups flour
½ teaspoon salt
1 tablespoon ginger
1 teaspoon cinnamon
¼ teaspoon nutmeg
½ cup sugar
1 egg
1 cup molasses

Preheat oven to 400°.

Cut the butter or shortening into cubes.

Dissolve the baking soda in the water.

Sift together the flour, salt and spices.

Insert STEEL BLADE. Using the on/off method, cream together the butter or shortening and the sugar. Insert FUNNEL. With the motor on, add the egg and molasses. Add the sifted dry ingredients alternately with the water and soda. Process just until the dry ingredients are incorporated. The dough will be soft.

Roll out to ¼-inch thickness. Cut with a cookie cutter. Bake on greased cookie sheets for 10 minutes.

Yields 2 dozen large or 4 dozen small cookies.

Peanut Butter Cookies

1¾ cups flour
1 teaspoon baking soda
½ teaspoon salt
1 cup peanuts (or ½ cup creamy peanut butter)
½ cup butter
½ cup granulated sugar
½ cup brown sugar, firmly packed
1 egg
¼ cup milk
1 teaspoon vanilla
Granulated sugar

Preheat oven to 375°.

Sift together the flour, baking soda and salt.

Insert STEEL BLADE. Process peanuts until smooth. Add the butter, ½ cup granulated sugar and the brown sugar, and process until creamy. Insert FUNNEL. Add the egg. Add the sifted dry ingredients alternately with the milk. Add the vanilla and give the blade another turn or two.

Shape into balls, roll in granulated sugar and place on ungreased cookie sheets. Bake for 10 to 12 minutes.

After the cookies have been baked, a small chocolate bit can be pressed into the center to decorate.

Yields 2 dozen.

Pineapple Delight

2 small fresh pineapples
1 lemon, rind and juice
1 cup sugar
1¼ cups unsweetened pineapple juice
¾ cups water
1½ cups heavy cream
¼ cup kirsch

Cut the pineapples in half lengthwise, leaving the green tops attached. Remove pineapple meat and hollow out the shells. Do not break the shells. Sprinkle the insides of the shells with a small amount of sugar and chill.

Insert STEEL BLADE. Using the on/off method, grate the lemon rind with the 1 cup sugar. Add the pineapple meat and continue to use the on/off method until the pineapple is crushed. Add the pineapple juice and water, and blend. Pour into a saucepan and bring to a boil. Boil for 5 minutes.

Keep STEEL BLADE in place. Insert FUNNEL. While the motor is on, pour in the pineapple mixture and puree. Add the lemon juice and mix. Remove mixture and chill for 30 minutes.

Insert STEEL BLADE. Whip the cream. Add the kirsch and the chilled pineapple mixture. Give the blade another turn or two. Spoon into the pineapple shells, mounding as high as possible. Chill.

For a touch of color, pour a small amount of Crimson Sauce (see page 94) over the top before serving.

6 servings.

Rhubarb Fool

1 cup brown sugar
2 tablespoons crystallized ginger
1 pound fresh strawberry rhubarb
2 cups heavy cream

Insert STEEL BLADE. Using the on/off method, mix together the sugar and crystallized ginger.

Insert SLICING DISK. Using heavy pressure, slice the rhubarb.

Turn mixture into a heavy saucepan. Cover and cook over low heat until rhubarb is tender.

Insert STEEL BLADE. Puree the rhubarb mixture. Set aside and cool.

Keep STEEL BLADE in place. Whip the cream until thick. Insert FUNNEL and, with the motor on, add the cooled rhubarb puree. Spoon into serving glasses. Chill.

Whole strawberries make a nice garnish.

8 servings.

Variations

Pureed strawberries, raspberries, apricots or other fruit can be substituted for the rhubarb.

Bread Pudding

8 slices stale bread
2 cups scalded milk
½ cup sugar
½ cup butter
2 eggs
½ teaspoon salt
½ teaspoon nutmeg
¼ teaspoon cinnamon
1 teaspoon vanilla

Preheat oven to 325°.

Insert STEEL BLADE. Using the on/off method, process bread until crumbs are made. Add to the scalded milk. Set aside and cool.

Keep STEEL BLADE in place. Using the on/off method, cream together the sugar and butter. Insert FUNNEL. Add the eggs, salt, nutmeg, cinnamon and vanilla. Process until well mixed. Add the bread crumbs and milk. Give the blade another turn or two.

Pour into a buttered 6-cup mold. Bake 1 hour. Serve with cream or Crimson Sauce (see page 94).

6-8 servings.

Steamed Blueberry Pudding

2 cups flour
4 teaspoons baking powder
1 teaspoon salt
2 cups sugar
1 tablespoon butter
¾ cup milk
2 teaspoons lemon juice
4 cups blueberries

Sift together the flour, baking powder and salt.

Insert STEEL BLADE. Using the on/off method, cream together the sugar and butter. Insert FUNNEL and add the sifted dry ingredients alternately with the milk. Add the lemon juice and the blueberries, and give the blade another turn or two.

Pour into a buttered 6-cup mold. Place in a steamer, cover tightly and steam 45 minutes. Insert a toothpick in the center—it will come out clean when done. Serve warm with cream.

6-8 servings.

Lemon Pudding Cake

1 lemon, rind and juice
¾ cup sugar
3 eggs, separated
3 tablespoons flour
¾ cup milk
½ teaspoon salt
1½ tablespoons butter

Preheat oven to 325°.

Zest the lemon, then juice it.

Insert STEEL BLADE. Using the on/off method, process lemon rind with the sugar until rind is finely chopped. Insert FUNNEL. Add the egg yolks and process until mixture is light and fluffy. Add the flour and milk. Process until well mixed. Set aside.

Keep STEEL BLADE in place. Beat the egg whites with the salt until stiff. Fold gently into the batter.

Butter a 1-quart soufflé dish. Pour batter into soufflé dish and bake for 1 hour, until set. Serve with Crimson Sauce (see page 94).

6 servings.

Fresh Peach Pie

Pastry for 9-inch 2-crust pie (see page 108)
6 to 8 firm ripe, medium-sized peaches
½ cup sugar
1/8 teaspoon salt
2 tablespoons tapioca or flour
2 tablespoons milk, or 2 tablespoons butter

Preheat oven to 450°.

Line a pie plate with half the pastry.

Cover the peaches with boiling water. Let stand 1 minute. Slip off the skins. Cut peaches in half and remove pits.

Insert SLICING DISK. Using heavy pressure, slice the peaches. Remove to pastry-lined pie plate.

Insert PLASTIC BLADE. Add the sugar, salt and tapioca or flour, and process until well mixed. Sprinkle over the peaches.

Cover with the top crust. Brush with milk or dot with butter. Bake for 10 minutes. Reduce heat to 350° and bake until golden, about 40 to 45 minutes longer.

Yields one 9-inch pie.

Potpourri

Salt

Vegetables such as
garlic
onion
celery
cabbage or
turnip
Kosher salt

Use a proportion of 50% vegetable and 50% salt. Insert STEEL BLADE. Using the on/off method, finely grind together. Turn into lidded jar and seal. Refrigerate 1 week without opening.

After 1 week of refrigeration, pour out onto a cookie sheet. Put the oven on its lowest setting. Bake several hours, until completely dry.

Insert STEEL BLADE. Process the salt to desired consistency. Store in a tightly sealed jar.

Good for pepping up gravies, soups and sauces.

Yorkshire Pudding

2 cups beef drippings
1 cup flour
¼ teaspoon salt
1 cup milk
2 eggs

Heat the beef drippings in a 450° oven. There should be about 1 inch of drippings in the pan.

Insert STEEL BLADE. Add the flour and salt and, with the motor on, add the milk. Process until a paste is made. Add 1 egg at a time and process until well blended.

Pour the batter into the hot beef drippings. Bake for 20 minutes. Reduce heat to 350° and bake 10 minutes longer. Cut into squares and serve with roast beef.

4 servings.

Curry Powder

5 tablespoons mustard seeds
8 teaspoons ginger
5 teaspoons Tellicherry pepper
1½ teaspoons cayenne
½ teaspoon cinnamon
½ teaspoon cumin
½ teaspoon cardamom
½ teaspoon turmeric
¼ teaspoon paprika

Insert STEEL BLADE. Using the on/off method, finely grind together all the ingredients. Store in an airtight container.

Yields ½ cup.

Sauerkraut

1 large head cabbage
1 teaspoon sugar for each quart jar
1 teaspoon salt for each quart jar
Boiling water

Insert SLICING DISK. Using light pressure, slice the cabbage.

Pack cabbage tightly into sterilized quart jars. Add 1 teaspoon sugar and 1 teaspoon salt to each jar. Fill jars slowly with boiling water. Add a sprig of dill and seal tightly. Store out of a draft for 6 weeks.

Rinse, put in a saucepan with cold water and cook over medium heat until soft.

Quiche Pastry Shell

1½ cups flour
½ teaspoon salt
½ cup butter or shortening
1 egg
3 tablespoons cold water

Sift together the flour and salt.

Cut the butter or shortening into cubes.

Insert STEEL BLADE. Using the on/off method, cut the butter or shortening into the sifted dry ingredients until mixture is the consistency of coarse meal. Add the egg and water, and process until a ball forms above the blade. Do not overprocess or the crust will be tough.

Roll out on a floured board.

Method 1. Line a pie plate with the pastry. Partially bake the crust in a preheated 400° oven for 10 minutes.

Method 2. Line a pie plate with the pastry and put it in the freezer while preparing the quiche filling. Fill the shell and bake quiche.

Yields one 9-inch shell.

Banana Chutney

1 large green apple
1 medium onion
3 large ripe bananas
1/3 cup golden raisins
1 cup orange juice
1/3 cup vinegar
½ cup dark brown sugar
1 tablespoon crystallized sugar
½ teaspoon salt
Dash of cayenne

Peel the apple if waxed. Cut it in half and core.

Insert STEEL BLADE. Using the on/off method, finely chop together the apple and onion.

Insert SLICING DISK and FUNNEL. Using heavy pressure, slice the bananas.

Place apple, onion and bananas in a large saucepan. Add the remaining ingredients and bring to a boil. Reduce heat to low and simmer for 1 to 2 hours. Cool, then chill. Serve with any curry dish.

Yields 3 cups.

Seasoned Bread Crumbs

1 loaf bread (1 pound)
2 tablespoons grated Romano cheese
2 tablespoons dried basil
2 tablespoons fresh Italian parsley
2 tablespoons dried oregano
1 teaspoon dried rosemary

Insert PLASTIC BLADE. Process the bread until crumbs are made and add the remaining ingredients. Mix well and store in a dry place.

dex